WITHDRAWN

Twayne's United States Authors Series

Sylvia E. Bowman, *Editor*

INDIANA UNIVERSITY

Maxwell Bodenheim

MAXWELL BODENHEIM

By JACK B. MOORE

University of South Florida

 **156**

Twayne Publishers, Inc.   ::   New York

TO THE MEMORY OF MY FATHER

Preface

THE career of Maxwell Bodenheim is one of the strangest in the annals of American literature, and his death surely one of the most bizarre. Though, as a young man, he was a highly regarded figure in post-World War I letters, by the time he was murdered in 1954 he was known, if at all, as a curious, sodden vestige of the wild days of Greenwich Village. Few remembered the promise and brightness of his art, but all who read the popular press knew about the bum he had become. Then after his death, again in the press, a legendary Bodenheim reappeared, the last of the great bohemians, the ur-Beat, the bourgeois shocker. The old anecdotes were rehashed, erotic episodes retold, sometimes with a fragment of a poem quoted, or a novel mentioned, such as *Naked on Roller Skates*. And everybody, it seemed, remembered buying a wretched poem from the old man for a shot of cheap whiskey.

The purpose of the present book is to present as accurately as possible who Bodenheim really was, what the actual events of his life were; and to describe, analyze, and evaluate what he really wrote. His (partly self-) victimized life as an American and American writer is significant enough to warrant telling accurately for the first time, even though briefly, to fit into the plan of Twayne's United States Authors Series. His poetry and fiction are interesting enough to justify extended criticism.

Although I have focused most frequently upon what he wrote, I have throughout tried to indicate the chief events of his life as I have been able to piece them together, and to analyze that strange life to see how this undeniably talented person took so many wrong turns in his course of slow self-destruction. I have also attempted to rehabilitate his early reputation as a creative writer and critic, since it was at one time far higher than most readers today realize.

I have quoted extensively from his fiction and poetry because I am dealing with material foreign to most readers and difficult to locate. I give enough plot to orient the reader to the discussion of characters, themes, and techniques that follow. The poetry is examined, as is the fiction, chronologically, volume by volume. Since Bodenheim had more definite attitudes toward his poetry than toward his fiction, I include a discussion of his concept of that genre. The general nature of each poetry volume is indicated by analyses of representative poems. After rereading the section on poetry, I feel I have made many poems seem easier than they actually are. For strategic reasons I have often cheerfully written equivalents of "is" or "means" when I should probably have stated "seems," or "might be" or "could mean." Recurrent elements in both the fiction and poetry are, of course, noted.

Throughout the book I have silently corrected what seemed obvious typographical errors in Bodenheim's texts. When possible, I used the *Selected Poems* version of individual poetry texts; otherwise, the original edition version. Occasionally I refer to both.

Since an extended published treatment of Bodenheim's life and works is nonexistent, I have relied greatly on interviews and documents supplied by people who knew Bodenheim or had bits of unpublished material about him. Bodenheim's first wife, Minna, was of incalculable help to me; and Bodenheim's old friends Louis Grudin and Conrad Aiken have been similarly kind. I would also like to thank for aiding me Doris Alexander, Deming Brown, Martin Bush, Allen Churchill, Floyd Dell, Donald Friede, Horace Gregory, George Kendall, Douglas Moore, Al Robert, Dennis Robison, Louis Untermeyer, and Emily Wallace. My colleague Elton Smith read parts of the manuscript and saved me from many errors of phrase and fact. Edward DeVoe's fine dissertation saved me untold hours of labor. I would also like to thank those interviewed who did not want their names used.

JACK B. MOORE

University of South Florida

Contents

Contents

Chronology

1892   Maxwell Bodenheim born May 26 in Hermanville, Mississippi. Lived in and around Hermanville and Memphis, Tennessee.

1900   (approximately) Family moved to Chicago.

1908/   Dismissed from high school before he completed educa-
1909   tion. Left home; joined army.

1910/   Attempted to be dismissed from army; ultimately jailed
1911   for desertion.

1911/   Bummed around Southwest.
1912

1914   Poems first published in *Poetry* and *The Little Review*. Part of Chicago literary revival that included Ben Hecht, Sherwood Anderson, and others.

1915–   Left Chicago for New York; lived with Alfred Kreymborg;
1916   worked with *Others* group.

1917   Provincetown Players performed his *Knot Holes* and *The Gentle Furniture Shop*.

1918   Married in New York to Minna Schein. First book of poems, *Minna and Myself*, published.

1920   First trip to England, where son Solbert was born. *Advice*.

1921   First stay at the MacDowell Colony, where he stayed also part of the summers of 1922, 1923, and 1925.

1922   *Introducing Irony*.

1923   First novel, *Blackguard*. *Against This Age* and *The Sardonic Arm*.

1923–   Worked for Ben Hecht's *Chicago Literary Times*.
1924

1924   *Crazy Man*.

1925   *Replenishing Jessica*.

1925–   Trial on suppression of *Replenishing Jessica* for alleged
1926   indecency. Book finally cleared of all charges.

1926   *Ninth Avenue*.

1927   *Returning to Emotion*.

1928   *The King of Spain* and *Georgie May*.

1929 *Sixty Seconds.*

1930 *Bringing Jazz!* and *A Virtuous Girl. Naked on Roller Skates,* last Bodenheim book to make a profit, also published.

1931 *Duke Herring.* Last trip to Europe.

1932 *Run, Sheep, Run* and *6 A.M.*

1933 *New York Madness.*

1934 *Slow Vision.* Bodenheim traveled to California for health and to try to sell his books to screen. From this time to his death, Bodenheim sporadically indigent; when back in New York, kept himself (mostly in alcohol) by selling poems directly to passers-by.

1935 Complained to New York City officials about inadequacy of relief money. With other writers marched on City Hall.

1938 Divorced by Minna.

1939 Married Grace Finan. Received *Poetry Magazine's* Oscar Blumenthal Award.

1940 Fired from Federal Writer's Project for alleged Communist activities.

1942 *Lights in the Valley* published. Appeared in William Saroyan's play *Across the Board on Tomorrow Morning.*

1944 Symposium *Seven Poets in Search of an Answer* published.

1946 *Selected Poems.*

1950 Wife Grace died after long illness.

1951 Married Ruth Fagan.

1952 Arrested in New York City for vagrancy. Traveled with Ruth to Chicago for reunion commemorating Chicago literary revival; disgraced self.

1954 Brutally murdered in New York City.

CHAPTER *1*

Preparations for Disaster

THOUGH many accounts list varying dates and places of birth, Maxwell Bodenheim was born on May 26, 1892, in Hermanville, Mississippi. No legal record of his birth exists, and his family Bible (where Hebrew faces French on each page) records the year as 1893. The number "3" was, however, written later over an erasure; and Bodenheim considered 1892 his birth year. In the autobiographic poem "Simple Account of a Poet's Life" he gives his birthdate as 1892, and he told his wife Minna that he was twenty-six at the time of their marriage in November, 1918. The confusion over when and where he was born is emblematic of Bodenheim's strange life, which culminated in his 1954 skid-row murder. At one time recognized as one of America's most important young poets, he sought disaster as surely and fervently as he pursued his art. Somewhere behind his masks of artist, self-destroyer, and bum, his real identity is hidden.[1]

Hermanville, a small southwest Mississippi town, was founded by Bodenheim's maternal uncle, M. B. Herman. The example of the respected uncle's fortunes burdened both Bodenheim and his father Solomon. Herman, the onetime drug, drygoods, and grocery merchant, appeared to them as would brother Ben to Willy Loman, when Ben walked from the jungle a rich man. Herman prospered after buying property and establishing stores where he knew the Jackson to Natchez trunk of the Illinois Central Railroad would meet the local crossroads. Eventually, this eminently successful Alsatian Jew studied medicine in Louisville and became a distinguished surgeon at Memphis' St. Mercy Hospital. He was a cruel comparison to Solomon Bodenheimer who also emigrated from Alsace, opened a store in Hermanville, was a traveling whiskey salesman, clothing-store clerk, and invariably

a failure. The father's lack of success was not ignored by Bodenheim's mother, Caroline (Carrie) Herman, whose brothers and
sisters continued to live well in and around Memphis, where several of the brothers were also doctors.

Carrie and Solomon Bodenheimer had only one child, born
when Carrie was thirty-three. Thereafter the graph of their existence curved downward, shaken occasionally by bitter quarrels
(or what Bodenheim thought of as such); economic defeat; and
job-shifts, changes in locale between Hermanville and Memphis
and finally Chicago, where their line simply disappears. By the
time Maxwell was ten and living in Chicago, the pattern of family
life was clear, if not the specific events. The father apparently
loved his son; but, harassed by his own business failures he was
unable to manifest his love. The strong-willed mother, chilled by
relentless financial decline and by the father's softness and lack
of drive in business, sharpened her dissatisfaction by prodding
both father and son into untenable positions. But Solomon, who
had only a proven lack of business ability to offer the American
dream of material success, continued to let Carrie dominate him,
though apparently never enough to seek aid from Dr. Herman or
any of his family.

As a result of his family environment, Bodenheim's childhood
was a disaster he never recovered from. His family's economic
decline, his mother's sharp dissatisfactions, and his father's failures as parent and provider contributed warping pressures. As
he developed intellectually and emotionally, he seems never to
have possessed the equipment psychologically necessary to live
with even minimal security in the ordinary confines of society.
Throughout his life he could not hold on to the numerous oppor-
tunities he had for success as a family member or as a writer. He
and his first wife loved each other greatly; he would have a son;
he attracted the friendship of many artists and the attention of
the serious critics of his day. Several of his novels were financial
successes. But as a success, Bodenheim was his father's child.

Bodenheim rejected the world that he saw his parents aspire
to, the close-knit Jewish middle-class world bound by established
social traditions. To him, this life was both harsh and barren, and
its authority irrelevant. Rebellion and rejection are obligatory
stages in self-fulfillment for Bodenheim and for many of his fic-

tional protagonists: for example, the heroes of *Blackguard, A Virtuous Girl,* and *Ninth Avenue* seek richer lives through violently rejecting their parents. Many of Bodenheim's books demonstrate that submission to authority—parental, familial, social, artistic, political—means in general submission to hypocritical forces and constitutes character weakness.

Yet Bodenheim clearly wanted to find the family and authority he was not equipped to accept. Flight and search showed itself, as Floyd Dell suggested to me, in his often bitter outcries against those who befriended and helped him most. His Communist fellow-traveling also reveals his split desires; for, as a radical, he adhered at least temporarily to an ideology seeking to destroy the established American society. He belonged to an authoritarian discipline whose goal was to remove the status quo authority.

When his parents wanted him to become a productive member of their middle-class culture, the young Bodenheim rebelled by escaping into dreamy art. His first poems, alluded to in *Blackguard,* were adolescent exercises in escapism. His life—as he later wrote of another character in *New York Madness*—"was the old story of a non-conformist, a recalcitrant and a dreamer, springing from dictatorial, materialistic, Jewish parents, who could not tolerate the idea that [he] was utterly different from their own much-prized cautions and repressions." Bodenheim felt guilty about his rebellion: the egocentric child sees even his parent's failures as his fault. Bodenheim's most autobiographical heroes in *Blackguard* and *Sixty Seconds* are criminals, and in the second book the criminal-hero is executed: Bodenheim always paid for his rebellions. His disregard of normal social patterns and responsibilities eventually ended his first marriage and led to his tragic third. His disregard of authority and tradition also isolated him from artistic and personal roots to a degree amazing in an era of the artist as solitary. And his self-inflicted punishments ended only in that final dreary alcoholic room inhabited by himself and two ex-mental patients, one of them murderous.

That room was in the distant future, however, for the bright rebel. In Chicago, as a boy, Bodenheim attended Hyde Park High School, on the South Side; but he was expelled for an undisclosed infraction. Biographic detail on Bodenheim's late adolescence is virtually nonexistent, but in *Blackguard* he indicates that his pose of arrogant isolation alienated most of his schoolmates, except a few girls. Nowhere in his published work or in private communication does he indicate any close friendship with a particular "chum." Nor did he belong to any gangs. He was a loner who wrote poetry and seemingly reveled in aloofness.

Later, when he wrote of adolescence, he returned again and again—as in A Virtuous Girl—to sex as the primary act of rebellion and self-assertion. In Ninth Avenue, the parents discover the promiscuity and this occasions harsh punishment; the heroine of A Virtuous Girl is harshly accused twice, once by her parents and once by relatives. Possibly as a youth Bodenheim flaunted his free sexuality; possibly he was caught in some sexual offense and punished—or perhaps he knew he would be punished for what he frequently proclaimed later as healthy animal activity. But the self-inflicted punishment his adult sexual peccability brought upon him is not conjectural.

Sometime around 1908 he ran away from home and joined the army. Today such a clear misfit would early be weeded out of the armed forces. After he joined, his compulsive anti-authoritarianism met only stern rule, which may have been his perverse reason for enlisting. Having escaped family, community, and religion (first changing his name from Bodenheimer to Bodenheim, and for the army to a name he never revealed), he attempted to escape from the army. He afterwards spread rumors to account for his desertion, and others sprung up around his legendary figure. Some stories portray him defending his religion against an anti-Semitic officer (after fighting Pancho Villa in Mexico!), and to William Carlos Williams he told the story related in Williams' Autobiography of Bodenheim's stuttered verbal triumph over a Marine interrogator: "You are uh uh uh no more than the sh sh sh shadow of a ma ma ma man." One of Ben Hecht's versions, in 1001 Afternoons, concludes with Bodenheim knocking a lieutenant over the head with his rifle.

What really happened is sadder and more understandable. Meeting for the first time a force he could neither fight nor reject, an absolute control, Bodenheim frantically ran away, was captured, panicked, and swallowed lye. This severely burned his tongue and eventually helped destroy his teeth (and probably accounts for his reported need for spicy condiments: he had little taste). The remainder of his tour of duty was spent at Fort Leavenworth. The army became another symbol of vicious authority until World War II, Bodenheim's only conservative period, when he also stopped the anti-Semitism he so sardonically displayed in novels and poems; wrote conventional verse instead of free forms; and sent letters to the *New York Daily News'* "Voice of the People" column supporting flag-waving patriotism.

I *"Home Is the Anti-Hero"*

But these shifts came long after his army experience. Following his discharge he wandered around the South; and, according to the pseudobiographical "The Poet Recalls, M. B.'s Merciless and Unedited Biography" in the *Chicago Literary Times,* he bummed for two years and was several times arrested as a vagrant. Bodenheim worked, so he claimed, one day during a rice harvest in Texas but was fired for being too slow. He also picked cotton, and learned to make a good profit by stealing cotton already picked and weighed, and presenting it as his own. He worked at this a month and a half, averaging better than two hundred and fifty pounds a day. He possibly visited his uncle Dr. M. B. Herman in Memphis, for whom he felt attraction and repulsion. Herman's portrait in *Blackguard* is relatively gentle; but poet and critic Louis Grudin, one of Bodenheim's closest friends, remembers that Bodenheim especially reviled Herman in his rare childhood reminiscences.

Sometime late in 1912 he returned to Chicago where he was employed in various unskilled tasks and was also a telephone lineman for a time. Soon he was known as a poet, not merely by personal longing, but by the acclamation of Chicago's intelligentsia. The period was Chicago's last flowering as a creatively original center, as Bernard Duffey shows in his definitive study *The Chicago Renaissance in American Letters.* Bodenheim wandered through Chicago's literary Bohemia as the incarnate terrible child: sarcastic, sardonic, ironic; he behaved disgracefully but was recognized as a young talent in the heady, liberal, amorphous society. All in all, he was accepted by his artistic betters and inferiors as a clever, obstreperous boy. Ben Hecht described him at the time, in *Gaily, Gaily,* as "a golden-haired youth with pale eyes and the look of a pensive Christ." As a poet Bodenheim was part of the renaissance but never a force; his talent for disorganization and his irresponsibility and his prickliness undermined his status as genius-manqué. And fairly soon—in 1915—he left the scene (a mutual parting that would occur later in his association with the Provincetown Players, and with the Pound-Lowell-Williams groups of rising poets). Bodenheim was often involved in the various artistic movements in his early days, but never at the very start and never quite long or significantly enough there to achieve any force; but for the time, in Chicago, he basked in the radiant glow of his accomplishments. He was acquanted with Floyd Dell, Arthur Davison Ficke, Witter Bynner, Edgar Lee Masters, Sherwood Anderson, John Cowper Powys, Edna Kenton, Theodore Dreiser, Eunice Tietjens, Carl Sandburg, and of course Ben Hecht.

Whatever the mutual attraction between the two, the relationship with Hecht was Bodenheim's most lasting, if not his most fortunate. In Hecht, he probably saw a more successful figure of himself—a madcap cynic, iconoclastic critic of public morality; a Jew who mocked Jewishness; and, at the same time, a man whose life was relatively orderly, who received the benefits of the materialistic and sentimental society he sneered at, who could even cynically manipulate (and this is true especially of Hecht's movie scenarios) the weaknesses and desires of the mocked society and profit in the very act of clearly sardonic manipulation. In his hard-boiled and witty film *The Scoundrel,* for example, Hecht thrust upon his audience a heavenly redemption scene, by then a tired device. Yet the movie's financial success proved the audience's acceptance of the treacle Hecht so gleefully served.

In Hecht, Bodenheim saw a man who enjoyed the best of several worlds: of art and license and freedom; and of society and safety and comfort. Hecht had the poise, the balance, Bodenheim lacked. He did not have to commit himself to a pose that could bring only disaster, just as he could operate as a kind of artist while cultivating bourgeois prosperity. Soliciting funds for Outer Mongolian Relief or writing scripts for Cecil B. DeMille, such as *The Greatest Show on Earth,* so that he could then write and live as he pleased; producing his own movies, or espousing Jewish independence when such a cause was unpopular—Hecht knew every moment what he was doing; but Bodenheim did not. Where one could survive in a carnival war against society, the other could not.

Until the poet's murder, Hecht continued to dribble money and attention to his friend. He was also capable of sending Bodenheim a telegram—replying to one of the poet's periodic pleas—saying he hoped the two hundred dollars got there all right; but, in fact, he never sent it. The prime formulator of the Bodenheim myth, he wrote a novel satirizing his friend, *Count Bruga*, that perpetuates some unseemly and inaccurate stories, and more recently in the play *Winkelberg* (1958), Hecht presented a nostalgic view of Bodenheim for which Hecht wrote his character's poetry because he didn't think the original good enough. In *A Child of the Century* (1954) he described Bodenheim as resembling "the Hoffman painting of Christ," and in *Gaily, Gaily* (1964) he places the same description in the mouth of a Bodenheim girl friend resembling Fedya Ramsay, the poet's onetime sweetheart whom Hecht supplies with an apparently fictional history. Hecht's friendship with the antagonistic Bodenheim was perhaps a mixed blessing for each.

In Chicago, when they were young, they plotted, caroused, and debated, before titillated literary societies, such issues as "Resolved: that people who attend literary debates are imbeciles." Bodenheim established the monotheme school, whose poets were permitted only one theme a month. At parties, he sometimes sucked smoke through a long bamboo pipe that led to a brass bowl, or he stuffed his corncob with what he called "nigger hair," or he disgracefully feigned seduction of exactly the wrong woman. One of his greatest talents was alienation, in which his artistry was sheer dazzling genius. But nothing was sacred to Bodenheim and Hecht, especially each other. For example, Bodenheim expanded a walk-on chorus in Hecht's play *Dregs,* when he was simply to stagger on stage in front of a saloon and sing "Every morn I bring her vi-o-lets," into a near opera of elaboration and repetition. But their differences seemed on the surface, and they later collaborated on other plays specifically intended for production in the Player's Workshop (1915), which they founded with "Princess" Lou Wall Moore.

Bodenheim met others in Chicago, sometimes at parties such

as those given by Margie Curry, when Sherwood Anderson read from his manuscript *Winesburg, Ohio;* or at the Vagabond Club, where he met Bill Haywood, leader of the Industrial Workers of the World. And Bodenheim was pointed out, noticed, remembered—if not for his art, for his performance. Sherwood Anderson remembered the corncob pipe; and Margaret Anderson of the *Little Review* the pipe's smell, and how carelessly the consciously unconcerned Bodenheim dressed (even worse than Rupert Brooke, she said). Over twenty years later a figure as foreign to literature as Emma Goldman recollected seeing Bodenheim as one of the Chicago sights.[2]

It was, of course, as a poet he was known; and for that poetry his eccentricities were excused. His discoverers were inevitably Harriet Monroe and Margaret Anderson, both of whom were proud to claim the honor of his art if not the responsibility for his behavior. "In nineteen-thirteen and fourteen," when *Poetry* was just beginning, Harriet Monroe later wrote,[3] "a blond youth used to appear at the office now and then, bearing innocent young rhymes written out in an incredibly large round babyish hand."[4] This most unpromising and forlorn-looking of all young poets, "hunted and haunted . . . half-starved and half ill," did not have then his "later audacity." Nor did Bodenheim have then his later skill, to judge from his self-criticism in *Blackguard,* where he claims to have destroyed all his earliest work. But what he could produce impressed Harriet Monroe, who first published him in *Poetry* in August, 1914; his work also impressed Margaret Anderson, his second editor.

Indeed, Lawrence Langner recollects a feud between the two over who was to publish him first.[5] Calling on Margaret Anderson, Langner reports her rushing to him blurting breathlessly "We have just discovered a new poet, probably one of the greatest in America, and now Harriet Monroe is trying to print one of his poems . . . to claim credit for his discovery before we publish him in the *Little Review.*" The next day Langner met Miss Monroe, who also "had just discovered a new genius in American poetry named Maxwell Bodenheim." The day after that, Langner met the genius himself, a "pink and white" young man. Bodenheim read a poem which Langner only later could appreciate, so excruciating was Bodenheim's delivery. The next time Langner heard Bodenheim was years later in New York, when at two o'clock in the morning, Bodenheim came crashing downstairs at Horace Liveright's house during a party.

Margaret Anderson, an insider to the renaissance in Chicago, could recollect years later without looking it up in her files a line from the first poem Bodenheim sent her.[6] She remembered the line "moon paint on a colorless house"; and she also recollected that, during the period she cranked out the *Little Review* in a tent near Chicago, Bodenheim and Hecht walked from the city and pinned their poems on a handy canvas flap.

II *"The Short, Happy Life"*

The poet and critic Alfred Kreymborg was one of many who read Bodenheim's *Poetry* and *Little Review* poems, and he began communicating with the younger man. Probably late in 1914—Kreymborg is vague on dates in his poetic memoir *Troubadour*—after "an exchange of poems and confidences," Bodenheim wrote that he was preparing to leave Chicago for New York to meet Kreymborg, "the one man who seemed to have genuine elements of friendship."[7] The victim of real or imagined snubs by the *Poetry–Little Review* crowd, Bodenheim regaled his host with stories of the gang back in Chicago who had, he said, only "paper babies," eccentrics like "Billy Saphier" who "wrote poetry and had founded the Vagabonds, but stubbornly insisted he was only a machinist." The wispy Bodenheim was installed with his broken arm and battered portmanteau in the room on Bank Street above Alfred and his wife Christine. These must have been happy months for Bodenheim, for Kreymborg was more compassionate than Hecht, more willing to hear his intricate tales of woe, and more appreciative of his poetic abilities. They later had a falling out—again over real or imagined snubs, to guess from Bodenheim's letters; but Kreymborg remained essentially loyal to Bodenheim, and delivered a touching oration at the poet's funeral.

Bodenheim's stay at Bank Street was happy partly because he occupied the role of child in the household. To pay for his demands in time and emotion, he had few responsibilities beyond simply being Max. And in the morning Christine would maternally adjust the disheveled young man's tie, brush his coat, and urge him to eat breakfast. Without realizing it, Kreymborg also played the parent's role in sheltering and sponsoring Bodenheim. Kreymborg was impressed by Bodenheim's youth, not by the age of his pose ("he spoke with the weariness of an aged man"), and by the fact that he was already so good a poet. Today all the poets who arrived about the same time as Bodenheim are considered of a generation, but in those years Bodenheim was one of the youngest poets of recognized stature. He was about twenty-two when he met Kreymborg; at that time Robert Frost was forty; Carl Sandburg, thirty-six; Vachel Lindsay, thirty-five; Ezra Pound, twenty-nine; T. S. Eliot, twenty-six; Robinson Jeffers, twenty-seven; Wallace Stevens, thirty-five; William Carlos Williams, thirty-one; and Marianne Moore, twenty-seven.

Naturally Bodenheim met all the local poets and intellectuals, and for a while behaved with relative propriety. Kreymborg reported:

When he was introduced to the others in a party of welcome on Bank Street, there was no greater pleasure than listening to Bogie [sic] and Marianne Moore spinning long, subtle thoughts in colloquy. The extreme heights were attained on both sides in an atmosphere of sheer detachment emphasized by the dignified references, "Mr. Bodenheim," "Miss Moore." Bogie's poems . . . were frankly admired in the crowd, and the poverty-stricken misanthrope, who hated nothing on earth as he hated Chicago and the *Poetry* crowd—the first of an endless series of antipathies—sunned himself in this admiration. He took it as a matter of course, but more than once betrayed the impression that he was about as happy as he could allow himself to be without neglecting to keep an eye on the disillusionment certain to follow.

The disillusionment was not immediate, however. Made one of the many editors of *Others,* he mingled as an equal with some of the best poets of his time. *Others,* one of the most significant little magazines (and later, anthologies) for the printing of the new verse, was organized mainly by Alfred Kreymborg shortly after *Glebe* (in which *Des Imagistes* was first published in America) folded, and the magazine's revolving editorship included Kreymborg and William Carlos Williams, Orrick Johns, Malcolm Cowley, and Bodenheim. The group met informally first at Grantwood, New Jersey, in what is called by Kreymborg "a shack . . . on the sunset slope of the palisades." The cabin was originally owned by the painter and photographer Man Ray and the writer Samuel Halpert, and in that brave old world it was rented for nine dollars a month. Together with occasional guests such as Marcel Duchamps and Conrad Aiken, the critics edited the magazine. Later, meetings were held in Greenwich Village.

According to William Troy the magazine stood for "a democracy of feeling rebelling against an aristocracy of form," but Ezra Pound called the effort "a harum-scarum vers libre American product, chiefly useful because it keeps 'Arriet [Monroe] from relapsing into the Nineties."[8] Whatever its esthetic accomplishments, the magazine provided Bodenheim a task and, for a while, an audience. William Carlos Williams wrote to Amy Lowell, shortly after the periodical's failure, that *Others* was valuable since it "held the future of such a man as Bodenheim in its palms, even if only for a short while."[9] Williams, also one of many socially connected with the group, held a party in the spring of 1916 at which Bodenheim acted his part of mordant young man, much to the amusement of Marcel Duchamps. At other gatherings, however, Bodenheim was just one of many poets who brought their own lunches; played ball; and, as Williams said in his *Letters*, "struggled to converse with each other."

Bodenheim worked at his job as editor. One of his discoveries was Hart Crane, then eighteen years old.[10] On September 28, 1917, Crane wrote his mother that "Maxwell Bodenheim called the other evening, complimented my poetry excessively, and has taken several pieces to the editor of *The Seven Arts* [James Oppenheim]. . . . Bodenheim is at the top of American poetry today . . . a first-class critic though, and I am proud to have his admiration and encouragement." Though Crane overstated Bodenheim's status, his admiration of Bodenheim and the help he offered were probably sincere. Bodenheim also offered to publish Crane's work in *Others* when it resumed, despite Kreymborg's disapproval of his poetry. Crane later grew beyond Bodenheim; for, writing to Gorham Munson in December, 1921, he reported that the *Dial* contained "an atrocious piece of dull nonsense by Bodenheim," "'Insanity"; and in March, 1927, he consoled himself and Allen Tate by boasting that "the ice is breaking—for both of us. . . .

What we do win in the way of intellectual territory is *solid*—it can't be knocked over by every wave that comes along—as could Masters, Bodenheim, Lindsay, etc."

While Bodenheim continued to publish poems in little magazines, quarterlies, and popular periodicals (*Others, Dial, Seven Arts, Yale Review, Smart Set*), he also wrote plays in the years 1916–19 while shuttling between Chicago, New York, and Boston. In Chicago, he worked with the Player's Workshop, which advertised that it gave first performances only—most of their plays were so experimental that one performance was usually enough. Harriet Monroe remembered "Bodenheim's brief tragedy of the cosmos, *Brown*," as being produced at a first performance.[11]

He also repeated the pattern of his artistic life in New York by working on the fringes of the Playwright's Theater (the acting arm of which was the Provincetown Players) not long after its inception in the summer of 1915. During the 1917–18 season, which opened with O'Neill's *The Long Voyage Home*, Bodenheim had two plays acted: *Knot Holes*, written with William Saphier, and his own *The Gentle Furniture Shop* (which in *Troubadour* Kreymborg claimed was later reprinted in the house organ of the "'Grand Rapids Furniture" people). The plays were performed from November 30 until December 4, along with O'Neill's "Ile." Bodenheim played the Sleepy Mayor in *Knot Holes* to publisher O. K. Liveright's Jaunty Bricklayer, and writers Alice Macdougal and Dorothy Upjohn played Ghosts. Apparently Bodenheim's acting had not improved since *Dregs*, for he was practically the only warm body not corralled several weeks later for the thirty-character cast of George Cram Cook's massive *The Athenian Women*. Bodenheim acted in nothing else the Players performed. His plays are too fragile for serious discussion, but at best they contain some inspired poetic "mush" that satirizes poetic dialogue. Today, they read like occasionally witty parodies of Expressionistic theater, and possibly that is what Bodenheim intended them to be.

Bodenheim met Eugene O'Neill at this time, and apparently the two were friendly until they drifted to other places.[12] Dorothy Day, later editor of the *Catholic Worker*, Bodenheim, and O'Neill often sat in a Village saloon, the "Hell Hole," and wrote round-robin verses. At the Hell Hole, O'Neill and Bodenheim also met the notorious Hudson Dusters, an underworld gang so fond of O'Neill that it offered to steal him an overcoat that it thought he needed. Though the gang was quaintly named—one member was called "Goo Goo" Knox—the members were brutal; and Bodenheim could have used them in his underworld descriptions. When Bodenheim later wrote in 1926 about O'Neill for one of the first *New Yorker* profiles, he claimed that O'Neill needed to experiment less and write more about the world he knew. He also claimed that O'Neill had told him that "the underworld and the creative upper-world would have to unite before the earth could become a safe and unhampered place for intelligent people."

These years before the 1920's also signaled several crucial beginnings and endings in Bodenheim's personal life. According to Minna Bodenheim, Fedya Ramsay, who became a tenth muse and platonic inspiration for Bodenheim, died in 1916. Little is known about Fedya, though Ben Hecht has some stories about a girl like Fedya in his journalistic reminiscences. Several facts are, however, clear: Bodenheim loved her deeply and loved her memory even more; he told Louis Grudin that her spirit gave him ideas for poems. She was six years older than Max at a time when six years were a good many, was more experienced, and could provide the mothering he needed. Bodenheim dedicated nearly all his poetry books to Fedya. She apparently came to represent to him the constant, completely understanding, inspiring, always loving woman and mother he could never find in life.

A member of Chicago little-theater groups and a dancer with the opera ballet, Fedya took a job touring to the Pacific Coast, where Bodenheim was to have joined her. Boarding the train that was to take him to her, Bodenheim read by chance a newspaper item telling of her death after a fall from a horse in Santa Barbara, California. The shock was so great that he apparently blacked out, to awaken several days later in a ditch. A variant of this blackout episode is in *Blackguard*, but Bodenheim told the story first to Minna, who was not particularly credulous about his life. She considered the story essentially true. As late as May 17, 1934, when Bodenheim made a desperate business trip to Los Angeles, he reported in a letter to Minna that he had visited Fedya's Santa Barbara grave.

By mid-1918 Bodenheim had also fallen out somewhat with the Kreymborg-*Others* group, feeling that they had conspired against him. He wrote to Conrad Aiken, complaining that he had been excluded from a series of poetry lectures in Chicago which included "every American modern poet of any size . . . with the *one* exception of myself." Though he courted non-alignment and isolation, the disengagement he won was usually accompanied by mild paranoia. The same letter states his reactions about being ignored:

It isn't pure egoism alone that incites me to anger, but also a weary nausea at the sheer, hypocritical effrontery and blandly benign masks which some people are capable of. Standing before their superhumanly adroit, never faltering smoothness and protestations of friendship, I feel the fascination of Trilby confronting a gang of Svengalis. The very people that secretly and intensely dislike you and slyly spare no means to injure you and your work, always meet you with an outstretched hand, [and] suave protestations of friendship.

By 1919 the split with Kreymborg was complete. When Kreymborg's marriage was breaking up, he and Christine, Kreymborg wrote in *Troubadour*, had again taken in Bodenheim "as a humanitarian thing to do, also because he amused them in their travail." But, in December Bodenheim revealed real or imagined Kreymborg slights to William Carlos Williams at Williams' home in Rutherford, New Jersey. Bodenheim asked from close friends, and ultimately from his first wife, more than anyone could ever give in tolerance and understanding. As a result, he alienated most of his acquaintances at one time or another. Apparently, no one could offer him as much in reality as the dead Fedya could in dream.

Bodenheim's first wife, Minna Schein, tried. A writer's secretary in 1918 and a native New Yorker, she met Bodenheim at a Village tearoom, and they were married not long after on November 22. She was attracted to him partly because he was interesting and helpless, and he to her because she was interesting, vivacious, and not helpless. A bright, small, pretty girl with lovely eyes and a fine mind, attracted to Bodenheim's literary talents but not worshipful of it, Minna was vital enough to match Max's energy—if not his wildness. She shuttled from New York to Chicago and back with him, or after him; uprooting herself, she found a job, bore with his losses, and watched him wander in search of the elusive job, friend, or good time. In Chicago she once held two jobs—one as secretary for the International Workers of the World and another as part-time waitress in order to fatten her scarecrow.[13]

They argued sometimes over Bodenheim's seeming inhumanity, his cold use of others' pain in his own art. Once Minna was appalled at Max's scrutiny of an old washerwoman that he sought to anatomize poetically. They argued over Max's independent behavior too, his irresponsibility to everything but art. Once late in their marriage, when money was scarce, he was offered a large sum by a popular magazine for tales of the notorious Village. Max, who considered this work a prostitution of his talents, refused. Minna understood; but, after the birth of their son Solbert in 1920, she could not always be with him, could not always change jobs, could not always pick up the pieces after him.

But for a while she was there to return to—embittered perhaps, but there. When he was not with her, he wrote letter after letter filled with extravagant lamentation, remorse, and accusation: "My unusually Dearest Minna, A tuesday sends its rain against my heart, and no letter from you. . . . A day without a letter from you is like an unexplained pause in the possibilities of an indiscreet fairy-tale. Tell me that you are counting stars while I am away. I would give a kingdom in future expression just to touch your cheek now."

He might travel from her to write, to carouse, sometimes to wench; but he still demanded her attention: "I have not heard from you for over a week now. . . . I am at least entitled to a line from you. . . . Whatever staggering difficulties may coerce your time, you should at least be able to drop me a line to ease my mind concerning your pennilessness. . . . I could no more forget you than slay myself. If I ask for a written line in return for my forlorn love and labors, I am surely not requesting too much."

The posturing is comical, yet Bodenheim depended upon contact with Minna to curb his drift toward anarchy of behavior. Even in the mid-1920's, during his most notorious erotic adventures, he wrote her asking to remain in her favor. "Love me always and very much, dear," he wrote May 7, 1924, from Chicago; "for I have nothing else to lean upon save the false 'adorations' of women who bore me or extend a faintly distracting amusement." He was determined to perform for the adoring girls who worshiped the Don Juan-poet but also to remind Minna of his act's emptiness. He craved reassurance about his importance as man and poet, and he sought confirmation sexually. But for many years Minna was the center of love and stability for him, especially after the birth of their son Solbert.

But her wifeliness both attracted and repelled him. Letter after letter told of his deep dependence on her, but she had to rear a child, and she could not depend on him. Irresponsible Max could not be the center of family life. He mailed or gave her money from various jobs and literary sales when he could. But she also had to work, for he was the artist. Unlike his own father, he would not or could not be tied to the wife and son he clearly loved. The freedom he quested for could not exist within family confines. Yet at the beginning of their marriage, Minna and Max had only the highest hopes. The War was over—a war which had not touched Bodenheim because his discharge was dishonorable and his separate peace had already been established.[14] She was bubbling and pretty and sensitive, and he was a young writer whose abilities were recognized by such disparate artists as Ezra Pound and Conrad Aiken.

Bodenheim was working with the *Others* group when he met Aiken in 1916, and after that he visited Aiken often in Boston. The first visit was, according to Aiken in letters to me, after Bodenheim had assisted John Coffey (the professional fur thief and ultimately the model for the hero of Bodenheim's *Crazy Man*) escape from Blackwell Island Jail. The three lunched together in Cambridge after the escape. Another summer Max, Minna, Coffey, and writers such as Louis Grudin and Louise Bogan stayed in an artist's colony of their own in South Yarmouth. When Aiken fictionalized the colony in *Conversation* (1940), he vividly described Bodenheim: "a dirty raincoat flung capelike over his round shoulders, the white face already sneering, the queer yellow head bare to the drizzle . . . the lashless blue eyes, smiling with an affection of cynicism which couldn't wholly conceal the essential beauty—though a wasted beauty—of the pallid ascetic face."

Bodenheim appreciated Aiken's affability and his seeming stability, but not his art. Bodenheim's view of contemporaries' art was generally antagonistic, and many could not separate his critical view from his personal ones. Aiken, however, was able to laugh about such remarks as the following in a letter from Bodenheim of April 7, 1918.

Dear Conrad, I don't agree with a single line of your review. But having guessed something of what you intended to say long before you said it, my sulky vanity has had time to gracefully fall asleep. . . . I still place you among *the three or four real friends* I possess, but I intend to write a series of articles attacking your critical viewpoints and general outlook on literature. Outside of an earnest desire to destroy your theories you will find nothing personal or egoistically agitated in these articles. I still love you, you old scallywag!

Aiken was intrigued by Bodenheim's cynicism and his poetry, and he regarded him warmly as a person. Late in 1918, when Bodenheim and a friend, Sonnenschein, went to Boston to escape the flu epidemic, Aiken nursed Bodenheim when he contracted the killing disease. Sonnenschein returned to New York City where he contracted flu and, after Bodenheim had rejoined him, died of pneumonia. Bodenheim and Aiken enjoyed many good times together. Aiken still remembers his old friend's delight the time he came upon Bodenheim at an *avant garde* Boston café; and Bodenheim said: "Conrad, aren't you a little out of your element here?" Aiken replied "Max, I take my element with me." Aiken also later praised Bodenheim's poetry in an astute review, balancing him with Edgar Lee Masters' "solid . . . precise . . . square" poetry. Bodenheim's work was "diaphanous," tenuous, and abstract. [15] Masters employed the "objective thing, and Bodenheim the quality of the thing." Aiken clearly favored Bodenheim's poetry.

III *"The Artist Arrives"*

Pound's critical reaction toward Bodenheim was more ambivalent. He regularly acknowledged Bodenheim's existence, which, though short of ecstatic praise, was often all a contemporary could expect from the god across the water. Writing to Harriet Monroe in 1915, Pound explained why he voted the *Poetry* prize to T. S. Eliot: "Bodenheim shows promise in some mss. he sent me, but he had nothing in this year's *Poetry,* and besides he is young enough to wait." Two years later he complained to Margaret Anderson that "Bodenheim has been on the grump ever since I was forced to tell him that I could not perceive much originality in his work. . . . He was commendable in the first place because he was trying to take more care of his actual wording than either Masters or Sandburg. In verse having no very marked or seductive cadence, no rhyme, no qualitative measure, the actual language must be fairly near to perfection."

The next year Pound wrote, again to Margaret Anderson, to scoff that "there appears to be nothing in America between professors and . . . Bodenheim. . . . Anemia of guts on one side and anemia of education on the other." Yet in 1920 he still praised Bodenheim in a letter to William Carlos Williams, when replying to Williams' brilliant and polemical *Kora in Hell* (which highly praised Bodenheim) with the question: "have you the adumbrations of intelligence enough to know that the critical faculty which can pick you and Bodenheim and [Mina] Loy out of the muck of liars and shame is of some use even to poetry in a country so utterly cursed?" And in 1927 he wrote to Harriet Monroe suggesting a sort of *Poetry* book-of-the-month club that would publish Bodenheim, Eliot, Sandburg, H. D., Williams, and himself. For the jury, he suggested Williams, Pound, and "Bodenheim . . . to keep it from getting dead and academic and ladylike."

As a critic of American literature and as a commentor on the American scene, Pound naturally had to recognize Bodenheim during the postwar and the 1920's period because of his literary output. Bodenheim wrote literary, esthetic, and sociological criticism for little and mass-circulation magazines, as well as poetry and, later, novels. Along the way he appeared in several well-advertised scandals and stories; and he wandered seeking the elusive job; a solid, high reputation; and inner peace—none of which he was ever satisfied that he found. While the quality and the quantity of his published work were considerable, he never became more secure, nor more responsible or stable. He could not retain either money or job for any significant time; he could not stop insulting enemies or friends; he could not halt the flow of his corrosive wit and acid personality. To himself, he never gained any higher stature than that of official renegade.

His first volume of verse, *Minna and Myself,* was published in 1918 by his friend and sometimes employer, Joe Kling, of the Pagan Publishing Company. Bodenheim urged Louis Untermeyer to write the introduction, claiming that Untermeyer's preface would insure publication. Untermeyer's prefatory remarks were guarded but generally complimentary. He was surprised that this was Bodenheim's first volume, for he had expected to see the collected works of such an established writer. He stated that, under Bodenheim's hands, "words . . . have unexpected growths: placid nouns and sober adjectives bear fantastic fruit." Untermeyer then briefly balanced the virtues and vices of the poems: "Sometimes he gets drunk with his own distillation, and reels between precosity and incoherence."

Untermeyer's judicious remarks represent much Bodenheim criticism: general rather than specific, the critiques lack full critical commitment, praise Bodenheim's unusual imagination but are concerned about his excesses. Yet Burton Rascoe's complaint in *A Bookman's Daybook* (1922) that Bodenheim's work met "a conspiracy of silence" does not seem justified. Recognition was general, and each volume he published was noticed: *Advice,* in 1920; *Introducing Irony,* 1922; *The Sardonic Arm,* 1923; and *Against This Age,* 1923. Then, after a four-year hiatus, during which Bodenheim helped edit the *Chicago Literary Times* (1923–24) and wrote four novels, he published *Returning to Emotion,* 1927; *The King of Spain,* 1928; and *Bringing Jazz!,* 1930.

Untermeyer's qualified praise was added to by other major critics. John Peale Bishop reported that Bodenheim in *Introducing Irony* had "performed with violent skill upon English speech," and "cultivated a small and quite private garden, where he weds orchids and gilliflowers, sprays the morning-glories with vitriol, sprinkles the grass with rust. . . . I heartily recommend the book to anyone the least interested in American poetry." Malcolm Cowley wrote of the same book, after imagining Bodenheim writing it wearing mandarin robes, that "his verse is Chinese . . .

in etiquette . . . being stilted, conventional to its own conventions, and formally bandaged in red tape." But Cowley hedged on final evaluation: "No poem attains a lyrical perfection (he has a contempt for lyricists) and no poem is without its excellences. . . . He is good and bad at once; brilliant and boring; awkward and skilful. He has all the insufferability of genius, and a very little of the genius which alone can justify it."

Occasionally, the evaluation of Bodenheim's work was high. Edward Sapir claimed that "if Mr. [Edwin Arlington] Robinson, Mr. [John Gould] Fletcher, Mr. Aiken, and Mr. Bodenheim are not the real aces [of American poetry], I still believe Mr. Bodenheim one of the four." Of *Bringing Jazz!*, Horace Gregory said it was one of but two successful attempts "to capture jazz rhythm with all its essentials intact and at the same time to create actual poetry." The other example was Eliot's "Fragments of an Agon: Wanna Go Home, Baby?"[16] Earlier, in the December, 1920 *Dial*, Stewart Mitchell contrasted *Advice* with an anthology of Wordsworth's poems! Wordsworth was an example of the old poet; Bodenheim, the new.

Bodenheim's poetry received, therefore, adequate recognition. If few critics offered unqualified praise, few went as far in the other direction as H. L. Mencken, who wrote to George Stirling that "there is no more poetry in the whole published work of Bodenheim than you will find in any average college yell."[17] Generally, those who could not praise him recognized his importance on the modern scene; Edmund Wilson even apologized for his lack of appreciation: "William Carlos Williams and Maxwell Bodenheim I have tried my best to admire, but I have never been able to believe in them."[18] (Wilson later remembered being characterized by Bodenheim as a "fatuous policeman, menacingly swinging his club.") Poet-critics were apt to be highest in their praise of Bodenheim's art—men like Gregory, Grudin, and Aiken. William Carlos Williams observed in his autobiography that "his poems were always colorful and their images sensitive and well observed."

The journalists also respected his talent, even if they did not claim him a genius: Burton Rascoe, then one of the country's most influential critics, in *A Bookman's Daybook* listed him as one of our "lyric poets of the first order since Poe"; and others on the list were Emily Dickinson, Sarah Teasdale, Arthur Ficke, Wallace Stevens, Sandburg, Lindsay, and Masters. And throughout the 1920's Bodenheim's name was known to even desultory readers of poetry. In William Stanley Braithwaite's *Anthology of American Verse* for 1926, a sort of official, standard recapitulation of modern American poetry, Bodenheim was discussed and at least grudgingly praised in three separate sections—in an article by Henry Harrison on Jewish poets—Harrison doesn't really like Bodenheim but admits him "in the first rank"; in a regional article by E. Merril Root who says the Chicago poet "has found his own restless brilliance, and is usually exciting, even though not excelling"; and in an article by Marianne Moore on "New Poetry Since 1912," in which he appears as one who "contributed to making respectable as poetry, verse which was not rhymed." Herbert Gorman's remarks in the *Saturday Review of Literature* for June 18, 1927, might stand as a résumé of Bodenheim criticism during the 1920's: "To consider Mr. Bodenheim at all is very much like considering a prickly pear; one never knows when he is going to get a thorn run through his finger. Still, like the prickly pear, once the combative surface is pierced, an edible and tasty (albeit faintly acidulous) fruit is to be discovered."

Although Bodenheim wrote twelve novels from 1923 to 1934, he was never very seriously considered as a novelist. He thought of himself first as a poet, and so did others. Criticism of his novels is not very intense, nor even conventionally complimentary. Reviewers generally found his books clumsy, tasteless, and too subjective.[19] The occasional good reviews, for example one on *Georgie May* in the *Bookman* for September, 1928, praised Bodenheim's bitter portrayal of modern society and its victims. "Her tragic figure stands forth with cruel clarity, drawn with ugly, sympathetic lines, poised on the brink of the stagnant pool which was her unavoidable fate. Destiny and Mr. Bodenheim connived to make Georgie May a helpless, defiant, pathetic, spirited victim of realistic circumstance."

The third literary role Bodenheim played during the 1920's was critic of contemporary issues. He published in nearly all the important periodicals of the time; and he usually wrote with interesting if idiosyncratic incisiveness, when he did not vaguely rhapsodize. He wrote essays for *New Republic, Dial, New Yorker,*

North American Review, American Mercury, Literary Review, Nation, Saturday Review of Literature, and for other smaller magazines. Brief discussion of a few of his essays should indicate his work's scope.

"Men and Women" combines anthropological insight with a Bodenheim bias to offer an antidote to Freudian psychology, for Freud was another authority figure he felt compelled to rebel against. Floyd Dell conjectured in a letter to me that Bodenheim was too proud of his own mysterious neuroses to have them explained away in conventional Freudian manner. Bodenheim claimed in his article that "no actual need has ever compelled man to be the hunter and master of woman, or woman to be the ruler of man, but the monotone of their sexual contact demanded an important masquerade." Bodenheim continued to argue for an element in man not admitted by Freudians—"the fire ringing the mud." Not necessarily the last word in psychoanalytic knowledge, the article displays Bodenheim's interesting advancement of arguable ideas, which is after all one aim of criticism.

In "Psychoanalysis and American Fiction," Bodenheim focused his anti-Freudian attack upon native literature, and incidentally informs us concerning his own fiction. He terms psychoanalysis "the spoiled child of a realistic age" whose "boisterous manners should be corrected by a metaphysical spanking. . . . The disciples of Freud," he claimed, "have changed his modest premise into the contention that sex underlies and dominates all human motives and is the basis of all creations." Bodenheim's minimizing of sex may seem strange to those who have seen his novels erroneously characterized as sex-ridden, which in totality they are not. The novels have also been characterized as sensational, which they are in totality not. Sex in his fiction at best symbolizes a basic kind of honest communication and at worst represents another form of hypocrisy, or an evil manifestation of authoritarian power. Even as communication, it can be transcended; it is a good when natural and free, but no more than a good.

In the article he claims that the misinterpretation of Freud has led to a society and literature dominated by sex, for "whenever man is particularly conscious of [failing] to conquer and discipline his flesh he engages in a wild effort to magnify and exalt its importance." American novels reflecting this "wild effort" Bodenheim divides into several classes: the "sensual melodrama, written in an awkwardly forced style and unsuccessfully wavering between Whitman and Baudelaire, such as Waldo Frank's *Rahab*"; "the novel in which sensuality adopts a heavy, clumsy and naively serious mien, such as the novels and stories of Sherwood Anderson"—and here he nicely characterizes Anderson at his worst—"in which young men lie upon their backs in cornfields and feel oppressed by their bodies." Bodenheim also vividly lists "the novel in which sensuality becomes half-flippant and half-sentimental, and plays the youthful ape to sophistication, such as the creations of F. Scott Fitzgerald," and "the novel in which sensuality, sordid and undressed, fights with longings for business success," as in Theodore Dreiser.

Occasionally, Bodenheim was a poetry critic. He tended to subjective impressionism and phrase-making, but his remarks are often to the point in knowledge, if not to the point in question. His remarks to "A. C. H." (Alice Corbin Henderson) in the June, 1919, *Poetry,* cogently demolish her objections to free verse; his *New Yorker* portrait of O'Neill offers the restrained advice that the playwright should perhaps return to the reality he knows rather than continue his constant experimentation; his remarks in the *Chicago Literary Times* on Eliot's *The Waste Land* state generally and vitriolically what some Eliot critics—such as Karl Shapiro—more quietly and precisely suggest: Bodenheim calls the work "intellect engaging in a drunken commotion, and erudition prattling with the husky candor of a vagrant in the back room of a saloon."[20] An article "On Literary Groups" for the *American Mercury* offers a less visceral view of American literary criticism in the 1920's. Bodenheim states that "critics are always hunting for two amusing phantoms—an 'awakening' of some kind and 'a spirit' attached to a region and voiced by its writers."

As a poet, novelist, and critic, Bodenheim was constantly before the literary audience with work of quantity and quality throughout the 1920's and into the 1930's. He made no large sums of money, and what he did make, quickly evaporated. He gained a few friends, and perhaps a disproportionate amount of notoriety. But he was recognized as a fixture on the literary scene in New York, Chicago, and overseas as well, primarily as poet, but also as a quirky man of letters.

CHAPTER *2*

Early Poetry and Fiction

WHILE Bodenheim has frequently been linked with the Imagists, he is in no exact sense one. Conrad Aiken recognized this fact as early as April 5, 1919, in an essay he wrote for *Dial*. After praising Bodenheim's "delicate precision of phrasing" and his subtle "pictorial" quality, Aiken warned that "it would be a great mistake to ticket Mr. Bodenheim as an Imagist." More recently he has characterized the poetry as an interesting "offshoot of Imagism."[1] Bodenheim's blossoming as a poet roughly coincides with that of Imagism's birth and sway, and many of the poets with whom he was friendly—William Carlos Williams, for example—are usually thought of as Imagists. But Bodenheim's art paralleled without ever really intersecting much of the Imagist poetry. He is, in fact, in many ways a curiously old-fashioned poet, so old-fashioned that he seemed clearly one of the most original poets of his day. He wrote like no one else around him, and surely no one after him wrote precisely as he did. He claimed upon his first publication in the *Little Review* in September, 1914, that he was "an intense admirer of Ezra Pound's. . . . I worship him"; but neither Pound nor any other contemporary influenced him more than generally. His own character, his stance, was stamped into every poem he wrote, for good or bad.

Bodenheim was a poet of sensibility, in the old sense of the word. Through an impressionistic, though often highly controlled, investigation of his emotional responses to the people and world about him, he apparently hoped to reveal to his audience the essential truths about those people and that world. As a poet, he left rational, objective surfaces of the mind and object unexposed; he preferred to scrutinize his own highly intense, highly personal world view. He rarely attempted to render accurately the thing in itself, but rather rhapsodized upon the emotional re-creation of the thing within himself. At his best, he achieved sparkling and remarkable insights; at his worst, a temporarily catchy vagueness or flat sentimentality. In his poetry, as in his novels and in his life, he shied from disciplined factuality and from responsibility to rational or recognized authority. In all things, Bodenheim was the measure.

He ordinarily did not emphasize Imagist aims: concreteness, simplicity, concentration, natural speech rhythms (though in one strange, personal way he did, for he came to speak as he wrote), colloquial diction, or firmly outlined images. Often his poems suggested rather than stated overtly; but this diffusion of thought results more from the difficulties involved in registering the individual strands of reaction evoked by the response to some object, idea, or person than from any desire to avoid telling the reader exactly what is being felt or described. He tended to mannerism in reporting his reactions, since he claimed that "originality, therefore, can only occur in the style and not the content of man's creations. In literature, the way in which a man shifts and contrast his words, and not what he actually says, determines his freshness."

And he constantly switched significance back from the thing observed to himself; for, as he wrote, "I deny that vision is any part of the poet's business. Let him leave that to the philosopher, novelist and political-economist—those people who are forever engaged in explaining and pigeon-holing life and individuals, and concern himself with the many, unrealized possibilities of word-combinations: possibilities by means of which he may discover adroitly hidden threads within himself and within the life about him. The luxury of looking ahead and pointing a confident finger at what in reality is but a plausible mirage, or of generalizing about an insoluble melée, is one that does not appeal to me."[2]

One of the complexities involved in reading Bodenheim's poetry—and elsewhere in the just quoted letter he stated his aim was a "delicate complexity"—stems from his theory. Naturally, he registers his own perception of an object or situation or emotion, so that the reader must be prepared to analyse not only the quality or final result of perception, but the emotional and intellectual lens through which Bodenheim perceives. That is, his response to what is outside himself is significant, but it is often meaningful only if the apparatus through which he responds is understood. Bodenheim did not clearly distinguish in his own mind between reality and illusion, and in his response to the real and the illusory he is apt to place both on the same plane of being.

To him, a thought, a color, and a sound are equally substantial—or insubstantial. When he refers in one of his early poems to a voice composed of "cool rubies of sound" in which the lover bathes, he is not speaking metaphorically since he is describing a feeling and not an objective reality. The various levels of sense and substance equally affect the poet's response and in that way are equally real and substantial. The imagined feeling of coolness, the imagined hard, beautiful ruby, the real sound of the voice, and the imagined cool wetness of bathing all merge into one emotionally actual response. To the reader this kind of imagery may be meaningless beyond what it vaguely suggests because it lacks visual or any other sensory concreteness. How can one bathe in rubies of sound? Synesthesia would explain bathing in sound, but not rubies of sound. What is even the figurative sense of rubies of sound?

Bodenheim does not always maintain consistency in recognizing levels and kinds of substances and essences that provoke a response within him. Such a poet as Shelley maintains remarkable control over the varying tangible and intangible objects and qualities imaged throughout the song from *Prometheus Unbound* beginning "My soul is an enchanted boat,/Which, like a sleeping swan doth float/Upon the silver waves of thy sweet singing." Shelley achieves a delicate but wholly recognizable balance between what is outward and what is inward, what is imagined and what is real. Bodenheim does not always achieve that balance and, moreover, does not seem to recognize the boundaries between variant sensuous and illusory perceptions. What would be synesthesia for another poet seems more for him simple expository comparison.

Bodenheim's poetic practice was drawn from his attitude toward reality. One of his closest friends, the poet Louis Grudin, writes:

The extreme Platonism of Max's imagery in speech as well as in his verse carried through to a total commitment, as in compulsive religious mania, a flight into systematic myth. It was as if Poe's cosmic parable of the verbal genesis of the physical world had possessed Max's mind. He believed inflexibly in the casual primacy of "intangibles," ideas and emotions were like individual persons to him, as autonomous realities within the "illusion" of the actual world. . . . A number of times Max solemnly confessed meetings with a woman he had once loved and who had died. . . . She kept trysts with him to hold long conversations in a language of pure poetry; and these were as actual as the visits of the Angel Gabriel who would come in person to pose for Blake. This was not feigned, and Max would be beside himself with rage when I hinted at skepticism.[3]

Concerning the poet's function, Bodenheim was of two minds. First, as already noted, the poet was honestly to report his response to the surrounding world of people and ideas. By fresh and original phrasing, he is to perceive "adroitly hidden threads within himself and within the life about him." He also claimed that "poetry has no utilitarian or instructive function."[4] But it is impossible not to watch throughout Bodenheim's poetry the delivering of various messages concerning how man should view himself and his world. His second volume of poetry is, after all, titled *Advice;* and, knowingly or not, he was constantly advising his readers, not always dogmatically perhaps, but nonetheless explaining to them many of the concepts directly promulgated in his novels. His early poetry then shows a second, perhaps unconscious function of the poet as a legislator of the world. His later poetry, when he becomes more and more politically involved, shows the poet as acknowledged legislator.

But even early in his career he tries to make the instructional poet compatible with the pure artist. The poet, he wrote in 1920, "exists to show other men what lies beneath their hard outer skin; to reveal to them the complexities and unfoldings which life has denied them." He admits that, with this concept of the poet, the writer is preaching; but the poet is "not a preacher in the ordinary sense of the word." The poet is "the mad, insulted preacher among men . . . one who indirectly tells men what they could have been, by holding his heart and mind up to them like an unconcerned child." The preaching is supposedly indirect, by display rather than by demand, and is performed with almost disregard for the audience.

Bodenheim sought purity of personal revelation, not of observation. This pure revelation was to portray for the reader in "bare words, expressions, forms, and colors of life . . . the nearest possible approach to the sum total of their essence."[5] The poet's expression tells only about itself, while indirectly engaging the reader's response to something similar within himself. And elsewhere Bodenheim praises the dispassionate eye that seeks poetry which "need have no direct connection with the salient motifs of human nature, and need only paint a picture without comment, or supplemented by the poet's purely spiritual reaction."[6] Interestingly enough, Bodenheim uses as an example of the dispassionate eye Walt Whitman, who was as involved with didactic poetry as was Bodenheim.

Bodenheim thought that through the "abstracted, impersonal glare of eyes that do not seek to judge, praise or blame," the poet would arrive at essential truths about men and their world. The presentation of such truths would not in itself constitute didactic poetry; for the artist was merely, through subjective analysis, arriving at ideal reality. The poet would not lecture his audience, but would try to approximate pure poetry, "the vibrant expression of everything clearly delicate and unattached with surface sentiment in the emotions of men toward themselves and nature."[7] But as will be seen, he was increasingly neither dispassionate nor uncommitted in his poetry—in some of his best poetry—as his reputation waned and as the economic system of the country buckled along with his personal resources.

I Minna and Myself (1918)

As the title to his first volume of poems suggests, young Bodenheim divides his attention in the volume between *Minna* and *Myself*. The poems to Minna are love poems anatomizing her physical presence and his emotions concerning her. The poems in the "Myself" section fall into four main categories: love poems, poems about death, poems of city life, and nature poems. Generally, Bodenheim does least well with nature poems. He is often clearly not concerned with the object to be described, but with his emotional reaction expressed in ingenious language. A tree or a flower, no more than glanced at or vaguely imagined in reverie, becomes an excuse for displaying the poet's verbal resources. Occasionally, though the phrasing itself is arresting, the original object of the poet's attention disappears beneath the superstructure of imagery.

"A Hillside Tree" is a good example of Bodenheim's nature poetry. While many of the separate images evoked by the tree are ingenious and impressionistically attractive, one realizes that Bodenheim isn't really writing about a specific tree at all, but perhaps about some vague, platonic concept of tree. Yet the only way the poem's imagery can be made meaningful rather than decorative *chinoiserie* is by recognizing the pathetic fallacy—the tree as person, or more specifically the tree as a bundle of emotions—upon which the poem is constructed. But it is difficult to juggle both the tree as concept and at the same time the tree as animal organism or animal emotion. The tree, Bodenheim writes, squats "like a drowsy, rain-browned saint." Its voice—not the sound produced by the wind blowing through its branches, but its voice "in which the wind takes no part,/Is like mists of music wedding each other." The wind is "a drunken, odor-laced peddler" bringing "golden-scarfed cities/Whose voices are swirls of bells burdened with summer;/And maidens whose hearts are galloping quests." Apparently while still squatting, the tree raises its branches to the sky "With a whisper that holds the smile you cannot shape." "You" is the tree, whom Bodenheim addresses in the second person.

As a mood piece, the poem is attractive, offering a foggy, dreamy, Oriental quality that almost narcotizes specific analysis of individual images. The morning scene, the wet brown tree blurred, the perhaps mist-muffled sounds of day, are portrayed with some skill. Several of the images do not function as they possibly should. That the morning wind is spicy and aromatic is not well connoted by calling it a "drunken, odor-laced peddler," whose smell surely would be rank. In describing the impression of sound the imagined distant cities produce, the phrase "bells burdened" is too heavy and dull with alliterated "b" and "d" sounds to function properly with "swirls." Finally, one must realize that the poem is a statement of how the poet feels. He is the poor but perhaps the sardonically smiling, rooted saint who hears distant life. And, if that is true, much of the poem's imagery is just decorative, rather than organic, since the metaphors relate to the tree while the emotion suggested is the poet's; and too many of the pretty metaphors don't relate to the poet's feeling.

"Intrusion," a better nature poem, is not so immediately clever. In it Bodenheim simply describes a field of lilies that "sag with rain-drops;/ Their petals hold fire that does not break out./ (As though it slept between cool vapor-silk/And could not burn.)" A "breeze stumbles" upon the lilies, stroking and spinning them. Bodenheim then explicitly relates his image to an emotional response: "The lilies and the young breeze are not unlike/ Your silence and the rush of soft words breaking it." He feels the same way toward the lilies and breeze as he does to the beloved. The poem's nature description is uncomplex and visually clear, as though the poet really knew what a field of lilies looks like. The application of the scene to the poet's beloved is also uncomplex and clear, and is attractively evocative of the poet's emotions. The loved one is fresh and beautiful as the lilies (whose biblical connotations are obvious), and she has a passion that is restrained but ready to flame. Like a lover, the breeze strokes the lilies into movement, and natural reserve is dissipated. The poet's emotional revelation evoked by the lilies is not added to the nature description, but evolves organically from his vision.

Bodenheim does not achieve in the poems of city life the power he later manifests, primarily because his overripe imagery softens the horror he aims to present: ugly city life is described too prettily for complete effectiveness. Of a streetwalker he writes in "Georgie May": "The ruins of your face were still twined with youth./ Vines of light questioned your face when you smiled./ Your eyes dissolved over distances/ And steeped the graves of many loves." In "Chorus Girl," he writes "Her voice was like rose-fragrance waltzing in the wind./ She seemed a shadow stained with shadow colors/ Swinging through waves of sunlight." In "Rear Porches of an Apartment Building" another city dweller is described in original but perhaps diffuse, overfanciful imagery calling attention to its own cleverness rather than portraying an object or emotion: "A sky that has never known sun, moon, or stars:/ A sky that is like an almost dead, kind face/ Would have the color of your eyes,/ O servant-girl singing of pear trees in the sun/ And scraping the yellow fruit you once picked/ When your lavender-white eyes were alive."

The difficulty in these poems seems not so much the poet's Oriental lack of involvement with his subject, his detachment— for in poetry non-involvement and detachment often bring their own rewards—but an ultimate murkiness of outline beyond the undoubtedly impressive use of metaphor. The wholesale synesthetic presentation of perception ends in fuzziness that obscures rather than reveals the girl's predicament. One senses that, like the thin man lurking within each fat man, inside the less effective of Bodenheim's rhapsodies exists the firm core of a better poem, if one could only get to it.

Such a better city poem is "Factory Girl," in which Bodenheim combines direct observation with sharp, meaningful images to produce the impression of a factory girl's eyes, and by synecdoche the worker's existence. The poem contains no pale roses, no tapestried decorations masking the bleak picture he wants to present. He begins with an image of destroyed natural vitality that mirrors the deadness of the girl's vision and existence: "Why are your eyes like dry brown flower-pods,/ Still gripped by the memory of the lost petals?/ I feel that if I touched them/ They would crumble to falling brown dust/ And you would stand with blindness revealed." The poet's distance, his detachment from his subject—for once again the object's significance lies in its reverberations within the poet's mind and emotions—is here organic to the poem. The dead, dried life of the girl is too brittle to withstand close scrutiny or handling. Such a life can only be observed, the poet implies, from a distance. Better not reveal anything of the girl to herself. Her life, the poet states, is "memorized. . . ./ Besides, in the making of boxes/ Sprinkled with crude forget-me-nots,/ One is curiously blessed if one's eyes are dead." Bodenheim employs fewer images than usual in the poem: flower imagery of dry pods and artificial forget-me-nots, dryness, life circumscribed by "high walls" and spent making boxes—thus reproducing walls—the color brown in brown pods and brown dust. Thus he illustrates his acceptance of the girl's own dumb, almost brutish, acceptance of her condition.

Several of the book's best poems are about old age and death. These reveal a young man's fascination with the subjects, and then tend to present death as an attractive or erotic power into which the individual pleasantly and even passively drifts, only to find himself ultimately overwhelmed. One of these poems, "Sharpness of Death," is in rough pattern like a "haiku"; but it does not follow that form's rigid metrical structure. The poem has two three-line stanzas, with each three lines comprised of a basic two-line image followed by a line of more or less direct comment. The first stanza portrays the passive drift into pleasant death: "A fan of smoke in the long, green-white revery of the sky,/ Slowly curls apart./ So shall I rise and widen out in the silence of air." The next stanza begins with an innocently pleasant image, but develops the idea that the individual is really attracted to death. "An old man runs down a little yellow road/ To an out-flung, white thicket uncovered by morning." The strange white thicket hints that all is not well, though it is too late to change course; for the poem rushes on: "So I shall swing to the white sharpness of death." There is in the last line the sudden bone chill that Emily Dickinson wrote about, in Bodenheim's image of all-engulfing white and in the unexpected and cutting "sharpness of death."

"Old Age" is another poem describing a gentle drift into death, but without the chill of "Sharpness of Death." The work begins with a series of simple images suggesting the poet's emotional state. "In me," he says, "is a little painted square/ Bordered by old shops, with gaudy awnings./ And before the shops sit smoking, open-bloused old men,/ Drinking Sunlight./ The old men are my thoughts." The poet says he comes to his thoughts each evening and quietly contemplates the passing scene, the "strong men, tinkling women, and dripping, squealing children" who stroll by. All is quiet, warm, muted, peaceful, as connoted in the nicely imaged old men, open-shirted, "drinking sunlight." These men may also represent the old thoughts who are in a real sense the only old friends the aged man might have. Even the blurry softness of such lines as "And [we] inhale scents from pale flowers in the center of the square" is functional, since the flowers of old men would be pale (weak, dying). "Inhale scents" is also more effective than the simpler "smell" because it indicates a kind of second-hand procedure, as though what was scented had to be artificially distilled, like the scent of perfume. The poem then ends abruptly with "Some evening I shall not return to my people." Naturally this line suggests death, and possibly that the ideas, thoughts, or emotions of the poet exist apart from the mind which is articulating them. The "old men" remain, only the poet will go to them no longer.

But Bodenheim's best poem on death in *Minna and Myself*, and one that he rarely bettered later, is the frequently anthologized "Death." Death is described as an exotic, beautiful, seductive, masculine force into whose sway one drifts as though hypnotized by a slave. Then, in a sudden switch of the last three lines, Death becomes a sinister power, no longer a slave but a master. In its progression, the work is reminiscent of Emily Dickinson's "Because I Could Not Stop For Death," but Bodenheim's imagery is more exotic. In both poems, Death seems at first attractive, almost politely seeking its subject. In both, the individual meets Death as though accidentally on a journey, and, in both, Death stops for the individual. Then Death continues politely to lure its object of desire along its journey, until finally the desired one is trapped by the seemingly obeisant fellow traveler. The point of view of both poems is in the first person.

Bodenheim begins with two direct, matter-of-fact descriptions which contrast to the exotic imagery of Death. "I shall walk down the road./ I shall turn and feel upon my feet/ The kisses of Death, like scented rain." Death throughout the poem is imaged as a Beardsleyan, luxuriantly erotic seeming-slave—all love, desire, and acquiescence until consummation. "For Death is a black slave with little silver birds/ Perched in a sleeping wreath upon his head." Death is at first an alluring creature beautifully decorated. But Bodenheim's apparent misplacing here of "'sleeping'" develops later into an accurate and alarming description. For the once-live silver birds are dead and exist only as the wreath Death has made of them. At first, though, the traveler develops only greater longing: "He will tell me, his voice like jewels/ Dropped into a satin bag,/ How he has tiptoed after me down the road,/ His heart made a dark whirlpool with longing for me." Several words here have interesting double connotations. The "voice like jewels/ dropped into a satin bag" connotes of course something rich, soft, and pleasantly smooth. But the smooth softness of the satin actually masks the hardness of the jewels. "Tiptoed" means to the traveler first that the slave is cautious, that he is hesitant to disturb the master. But it also indicates the stealth of Death's coming on, the secrecy with which the tricky slave operates. "Whirlpool" is attraction, but also a dark force entrapping what it sucks into its dominion.

The poem's final three lines clearly state the poet's growing apprehension about this beautiful male slave: "Then he will graze me with his hands/ And I shall be one of the sleeping silver birds/ Between the cold waves of his hair as he tiptoes on." "Graze" is a good visual and tactile word, representing a slight and in this context magical touch, a soft gesture of Death's hand in stunning sweep. It also perhaps recollects "glaze," an icily connotative word here that covers the same metaphoric ground as Dickinson's "gaze" in "fields of gazing grain." The slave has accomplished his desire, and the trap is sprung. Now master Death is cold, and the once object of longing is just another silver bird in Death's cold hair. Death then tiptoes on again, toward the next desired traveler.

The love poetry in *Minna and Myself* is best observed in "Poems to Minna," comprising twenty-seven free-verse poems relating to each other, as do the poems in a sonnet sequence or in a loosely constructed epithalamium. The work describes the thoughts and emotions of a lover observing his beloved between twilight and dawn. His musings, highly intense and personal, are dreamlike, as befits the nighttime reverie. The descriptions of Minna, mostly of her face and voice, are among Bodenheim's most mannered and synesthetic since, as the poet admits in the concluding stanza, the time of his observations is an interlude between real time.

Bodenheim first sets the clock time and the mood of his enraptured praise: "Twilight pushes down your eyes/ With shimmering, pregnant fingers/ That leave you covered with still-born touch." Apparently an argument has suddenly ceased, for "With little whips of dead words/ Silence cuts your lips to a keener red. . . ./ Night will soon whisk away this room/ But you are already invisible." The poet has entered, then, a trancelike state where the actual woman is transcended.

The poet now attempts to find metaphoric analogies suggesting his emotional response to Minna's face and body—an attempt that reoccurs throughout the work. The descriptions employ fancy, as opposed to the imagination, and tend to employ lush rather than sensuous imagery. The poem is never as physically abandoned as, say, the Song of Solomon. The beloved's "cheeks are spent diminuendos/ Sheering into the rose-veiled silence of your lips./ Your eyes are gossamer coquettes/ Tinged with the sparkling breath of discarded loves. . . ./ Your criss-crossed ring-lets of hair/ Are tipped with flattering opalescence." The poet also describes the night about him as it fuses in his emotions with his love for Minna: "'Moonlight bends over black silence,/ Making it bloom to wild-flowers of sound/ That only green things can hear./ A wind sprawls over an orchard,/ Frightening its silent litany to sound." Bodenheim was later critical of decorative and diffuse images in the poem. The *Selected Poems* (1946) cut several airy nothings. For example, Stanza XXII, which contained "The ever-lasting journey of your heart/ Gliding over a sleepy litany/ That winds through scattered star-flowers of regrets/ Is like a fragile traveller of sound," becomes later simply "The ever-lasting journey of your heart/ Is like a fragile traveller of sound."

The beloved is anatomized throughout the sequence, the world of love fancied. Occasionally, the poet speaks of prior loves that both have had, either imagined or real, and of the pain of love: "'Your limbs released fleeing andantes of pain"; and the pain of sex: "Our hands pressed serpentine pain into each other/ And stroked it away to twilights of relief." The sex act is also imaged and is portrayed as an act of emptying and renewal: "You are a well sprayed with cool rubies of sound/ In which I bathe and arise with another skin/ Like moonstone passion slyly courting/ The light breath of tired dream./ I drop my heart into the depths/ Of your disheveled serenity,/ And stroll off empty."

If the poem's images are sometimes vague, the organization of the sequence is skilled. Most of the individual stanzas are simply arranged. The first lines generally announce a basic metaphor, and the following lines develop the stanza's figurative and emotional potential. The total poem is rounded back to daylight and reality. Stanza XXV concludes the reverie proper, and stanzas XXVI and XXVII frame the dreamy monologue, announcing morning's arrival and the beloved's awakening. Stanza XXV itself begins by describing other lovers of another time, caught in faded pictures of halted love. These lovers are in a tomb: "Upon an arched sarcophagus of pain/ Are figures in arrested embraces/ With outlines so light we must bend close to see/ Old loves almost merging to one tone/ Of pale regret that hold/ The inner glisten of past weeping."

As the image is developed, the "arrested love" becomes associated with the poet's own love. Looking at other lost loves, he sees a possible reflection of his own. The embrace is his. The sarcophagus would naturally be placed in a tomb, and the room the poet is in has already in Stanza XV been called a tomb. Yet while the sarcophagus contains that which is dead—old loves—it is also a kind of immortality achieved through art, similar to the monument created in so many love sonnets. The poem itself is also then the sarcophagus, displaying the arrested embrace of mortal and immortal poet and beloved. At its conclusion, the stanza returns again to the sarcophagus image which now relates to the live lovers on their sarcophagus-bed, literally: "Our lips cling and our breaths wind to a hand/ With touch like summer mist/ Blending the arrested figures upon the arched sarcophagus of pain." In framing the poem with the sarcophagus image and in describing the arrested loves the artifact displays, Bodenheim incidentally parallels Keats's "Ode on a Grecian Urn." The stanza is like the other poems in *Minna and Myself*, for it is basically a work showing originality. The sequence "Poems to Minna" is also representative of Bodenheim's first book: at best, interesting and fanciful; at worst, fuzzy and uneven.

II Advice *(1920)*

Advice, Bodenheim's next book of poetry, contains no one poem as brilliant in its way as "Death," and no planned series as interesting as "Poems to Minna." The volume has, however, a solidity of accomplishment that progresses beyond the higher-flying but shorter-spanned talent of *Minna and Myself*. *Advice* contains, for example, a number of Bodenheim's best city poems portraying the sights and moods and people of the modern, industrial city. The greatest deficiency of *Advice* is unfortunately in the title series of poems. These comprise ten clearly related poems, placed sporadically throughout the book's first half, offering advice to some object or person.

Bodenheim is more interested in the opportunity for giving advice, and for suggesting the emotional reaction evoked within him by the object or person, than he is in observing what the entity advised really is and what its symbolic point of reference might be. Therefore, the resulting advice does not always seem to have any poetically logical connection to its ostensible subject. Bodenheim himself must have been uncertain of this relationship. One poem titled "Advice to a Street-Pavement" concludes originally "Only one who lies upon his back/ Can disregard the stars." In the *Selected Poems* he switches the advice to "Only one too long upon his back/ Can appreciate the stars above him." Worse, however, Bodenheim never overcomes a basic error of strategy indicated by the titles of some of the poems: he writes "Advice" to a bluebird, to a butterfly, to a buttercup, to a forest, to a grass blade, to maple trees, to a pool, and to a horned toad. Bodenheim was never particularly strong in nature poems anyway, but surely anyone presumptuously offering advice to a forest or grass blade should have some startling information; and advising butterflies and buttercups also seems a dubious proposition for a grown poet.

In "Advice to a Forest," representative of these poems, Bodenheim in communicating the mood evoked by response to a forest, describes the forest itself only indirectly; but he makes his own feelings apparent. Sometimes his phrasing hits upon imaginative if unvisual images: "Oh trees, to whom sunlight is a tattered pilgrim/ Counting his dreams within your hermitage/ And slipping down the road in twilight-robes;/ Oh trees, whose leaves make an incense of sound." Sometimes the images fall flat: "Oh trees, to whom the darkness is a child/ Scampering in and out of your long, green beards." The poet describes men coming into the forest to cut down the trees for planks, and the trees are requested to "Look down upon these children, then,/ With the aloof and weary intolerance/ That all still things possess." But the pathetic fallacy makes the poem silly. Trees would feel justifiably disturbed at unsparing woodsmen, though they have perhaps more to fear from poets. One remembers Joyce Kilmer's poem of course, and that of Bodenheim's contemporary, Max Michelson: "O brother tree! Tell to me, thy brother,/ The secret of thy life. . . ./ My heart drank a droplet of thy holy joy and wonder. . . ./

Reveal to me thy serene knowledge." Bodenheim, however, is writing about man, not trees. His poem says that man should be aloof and dispassionate; perhaps that the artist should not be moved by trivial carpers.

Bodenheim's two "Rattle-Snake Mountain" poems make far better imaginative use of nature, while indirectly offering advice, than do the "Advice" poems themselves. "Rattle-Snake Mountain Fable I" plays nicely and with no self-conscious pontification upon the folly of not being one's self, not adhering to one's own emotional makeup. The fable concerns a rabbit and a snake: "Rounded to a wide-eyed clownishness/ Crowned by the shifting bravado/ Of his long, brown ears,/ The rabbit peeked at the sky." He dreams of rambling boldly there: "To him, the sky seemed an angelic/ Pasture stripped to phantom tranquility,/ Where one could nibble thoughtfully./ He longed to leave his mild furtiveness/ And speak to a boldness puzzled by his flesh." Unlike E. A. Robinson's mild dreamer Miniver Cheevy, the rabbit acts; he leaps into the air . . . and crashes down into a snake who eats him meditatively. Now the snake inherits what it had destroyed; it is filled "With little, meek whispers of concern./ The crushed and peaceful rabbit's dream/ Cast a groping hush upon his blood." The poem ends with a coldly comic irony simply stated, without comment, much in the manner of Stephen Crane, whom Bodenheim admired: "In the end, his dry grey body/ Was scattered out upon the rock,/ Like a story that could not be told."

The second charming fable concerns a narcissistic squirrel who runs in treetops trying to reach the stars that appear to be caught there. High up, he looks down and sees in a pool "a handful of fairy nuts." He jumps for the reflection and drowns with "the fairy nuts . . . jigging over him,/ Like the unheard stirring of a poem." Bodenheim tells his fable of an artist who wants to hitch a wagon he doesn't have to stars that do not exist, with simplicity, though he employs a wonderfully elusive description of August air: "like an old priest/ Disrobing without embarrassment/ Before the dark and candid gaze of night."

Bodenheim also includes several sonnets in *Advice*, foreshadowing his later interest in that form. Mostly his poems reveal more interest in statement and phrasing than in techniques of sound, meter, or rhyme. While he achieves competence in forms other than free verse, his skill never lay in poetic architectonics. Even his free-verse poems do not experiment greatly with rhythm. His line tends to stop at some logical pause, at either a definite juncture or a slight, natural hesitation. To his credit, he features none of the artificial and now trite playing with word placement that dates so much bad, prosy free verse. He once stated in a letter to *Poetry* that he favored "organic" rhythm, "cohesion and fluidity" that imparts "escaping freshness and vitality." He also wrote that he opposed free verse that possessed only "an arbitrary musical flow which lures the emotions and thoughts of the poet into restricted areas of decorous triteness."[8] Even his sonnets lack "arbitrary musical flow." As in his free-verse poems, he emphasizes phrasing and idea, not sound.

The sonnets in *Advice*, one apparently to Ben Hecht, and one "To Orrick Johns" are competent without revealing technical brilliance. Both sonnets stress that the person described is a rebel, a cynic, or pagan; but neither man really understands himself under the mask projected to the world. The poem to Hecht was originally called "To a Friend," but in the *Selected Poems* it appears sadly as "To a Famous Friend." The work begins with some sharp images that eventually diffuse into vague metaphor: "Your head is steel cut into drooping lines/ That make a mask satirically meek./ Your face is like a tired devil weak/ From many vapid, unsought wines." The last line is weak itself, but it was still weaker originally when Bodenheim had "From many vague and unsought wines." The next four lines of the octave are not visual, but well suggest Hecht's nature: "The sullen skepticism of your eyes,/ Forever trying to transcend itself,/ Is often entered by a wistful elf/ Who sits naively unperturbed and wise." The sestet develops the picture of one whose cynicism tries unsuccessfully to get beyond mere negation, while never realizing the naïve youth hiding beneath the satyr's steel mask. The poem to Johns reveals the same unsparkling competence.

Several poems in *Advice* concern the poet and poetry. These reiterate what Bodenheim says elsewhere in prose with only slight qualification. In "The Mountebank Criticizes" (and Bodenheim is partly the mountebank, as he was a blackguard in his first novel), a colorfully impassioned poet rebukes those who blur the essential shape of life by portraying it coldly, in "greys, blacks, browns, and dull greens." These modern poets are too sober, too serious, too concerned with surface reality in their poems. When they take to colors, they "are ashamed,/ Like pages nibbling at a pilfered tart." The mountebank, who admits that his poetry is somewhat dishonest, confesses that "Pistols, perfumed rhapsodies over foul odors,/ Drugged and swindled the lustre of my time." Yet he also had a virtue; he brought color with him that "ravished our sorrow with brightness/ That often gave a lightness to our feet!"

"Dialogue Between a Past and Present Poet" makes much the same point in a dialogue. The past poet "wrote of roses on a woman's breast/ Glowing as though her blood/ Had welled out, stopping in spellbound intensity," to which the present poet charges "You raised an unhurried, often church-like escape./ You lingered in shimmering, pensive idleness." The debate continues, with neither poet really triumphing. Past poet argues that, while his verse blurred things it dared not view, his "towering simplicity" unloosed "a great evening of belief." Present poet counters that he does not shun reality, but he knows that "reality is a formless lure," and in his verse he attempts to untangle the colorless surface of life. Thus he approaches the "mountebank's" stand. The dialogue, and its unresolved outcome, clearly reflect two sides of Bodenheim's concept of poetry. His phrasing colors life, but his insights strip it bare, or try to.

The aims revealed in "Dialogue" are manifest in the city poems of *Advice*. In these Bodenheim, who achieves an often delicately imaged portrait of life in the deadening modern city, arrives at poetry akin to the Tender Realism of the Ashcan School in American painting so significant from about 1910. Paintings by any one of "The Eight"—John Sloan's "Six O'Clock" (1912), Robert Henri's "New York Street in Winter" (1902), or Everett Shinn's "Rush Hour, New York City" (1908)—are painterly precursors of Bodenheim's poems. And in the 1920's American artists again performed sometimes tender dissection on urban life, as in George Bellows' "Gramercy Park." The size, and crush, and loneliness of the city, all portrayed in Bodenheim's poems, were also depicted in paintings such as Reginald Marsh's "Subway," Georgia O'Keefe's "Skyscraper at Night," and Edward Hopper's "Automat." Bodenheim's poems could serve as texts for these works.

Bodenheim gives his impressions of New York and Chicago, of their streets and of those who walk along them, mostly the social underdogs: mill workers, Negroes, Jewish peddlers. Social indictment exists in the poems, but—as in the paintings mentioned—the indictment is often muted through a colorful, romanticized vision producing beauty. "South State Street: Chicago" depicts a drunken, cheap nighttown devoid of vitality: a world violent mostly in the squalid boredom it presses upon those dwarfed by its cold, impersonal buildings. Yet the street is described as through a mist blurring the shape of neon ugliness, as darkness fogs the dirty harshness of our cities: the poem is much like Sloan's "Six O'Clock."

Bodenheim's free verse begins with a general description of South State Street. Etherizing images prepare the reader for the dreamy view from which he will see the street's buildings and cheap romances: "Rows of blankly box-like buildings raise their sodden architecture/ Into the poised lyric of the sky." Thus the backdrop of the poem is set: the sweeping, free life above the city, the unattainable sky, and the attainable dull stupidity of entrapping city life with its repetitious, blank buildings that only mar the sky without ever really touching it. While standing at street level, one sees the strewn debris of urban existence, "pawnshops and burlesque theatres" that "yawn beneath their livid confetti"; everything is scrambled together, "cut-glass bowls, and satchels . . . slyly shaded cabarets." At first, no color brightens the street, all is black, "livid." Bodenheim's description reveals no cruel opponent, just stony indifference.

"Wander with me down this street," the poet asks in the second stanza. But the poet is no Prufrock, for he does not live in this city. He sees it, feels it, but is never a part of it, except as the imagination re-creates in what it sees, shapes already within itself: the poet gives form and substance to the world he says he sees. He gives snapshots of several street people who are all contiguous, yet unable to achieve contact beyond self. All search but none find. A woman stands "Sleekly, sulkily complacent,/ Like a tigress nibbling bits of sugar," next to a "brawny, white-faced man/ [Who] searches for one face amidst the crowd." He almost touches a "snowy girl/ Whose body blooms with cool withdrawal," and she stares unseeing into the crowd. Then two pairs of girls—two factory workers and two "languid girls"—move through the crowd with searching impudence, "the pride of breasts and hips." The section concludes depressingly with the image of a drunken woman lurching from a bar and indifferently brushing past an old bum whose "thin arm leaps out/ And hangs a moment in the air,/ As though he raised a violin of hate/ And lacked the strength to play it." Even the contact of hate is too much to achieve on the street.

Suddenly in Section III the people of the street spring into mechanical, relentless rhythms of driven masses. Bodenheim switches to a dominantly trochaic line and employs one heavy masculine rhyme to echo the developing lock-step force of the "endless crowd" that "Pounds its searching chant of feet/ Down this tawdrily resplendent street." The mass strays into a burlesque house "Framed with blankly rotund girls," and disintegrates into separate individuals. Bodenheim breaks the basic trochaic and heavy rhythm to describe the agility of one "burly cattle-raiser" who walks "With the grace of windswept prairie grass." Next to him are more typical street citizens, a "stolid, doll-like girl" and a "heavy youth" who "Dully stands beneath his bluffing mask."

Then Bodenheim cuts to a cabaret. Here at first is seeming gaiety, "Mutely twinkling fragments of a romance. . . ./ Men and women, jovially emboldened." The cabaret fades into a "strange pastoral" peopled garishly with "Hectic shepherdesses drunk with night" whose laughter is "like softly brazen cowbells." The women mingle coquettishly in "mincing colors" and then suddenly the mock-pastoral dissolves back into saloon. What was gay is cheap and violent: a man "hurtles out/ From the doorway's blazing pallor,/ Smashing into the drab sidewalk./ His drunken lips and eyelids break apart/ Like a clown in sudden suicide." Then the poet-observer draws back from the "mottled nakedness/ Of the scene," and all people vanish from the street. Like a ballet stage empty of dancers, only the dark road and a few lingering discordant sounds remain: "Stoically crushed in hovering grey,/ Night lies coldly on this street./ Momentary sounds crash into night/ Like spectral curses stifled after birth." The poem ends with a final ironic return to the surrounding, inescapable trap, the buildings dwarfing the street and pointing to an unattainable freedom: "And over all the blankly box-like buildings/ Raise their sodden architecture/ Into the poised lyric of the sky." Bodenheim's well-orchestrated poem circles back to its start, for the poet and reader begin and end with the sky that no one on the street ever notices.

Bodenheim corroborates and reinforces his image of the city and its people in several other poems. Repeatedly, he emphasizes the mute acceptance, even the submissiveness of the city dweller. In "East Side: New York" he describes "An old Jew [who] munches an apple," whose oddly tender mouth, "Like that of a whistling girl," is haunted by "Hopes that lie within their graves/ Of submissive sternness." Negro "Foundry-Workers" flash their arms "Into a glistening frenzy of motion," but their "thoughts are smashed into a dejected trance." The men from the "Steel-Mills: South Chicago" seek escape from man-crushing mills with a prostitute with "something of a village" about her; but always they return to the mill "Upon their lips a limply child-like surrender." Chicago or New York, "South-State Street," or "Broadway," urban life brings no real change for good.

In 1920 the Bodenheims sought change in England. Continental life looked exciting and inexpensive, as Malcolm Cowley's *Exile's Return* documents; and Bodenheim also trailed some elusive job that would have guaranteed his nascent family's security. Since he had no money for travel, he tried to borrow. Louis Untermeyer turned him down: he had loaned Bodenheim several sums before. As another who aided Bodenheim (and wishes to remain unnamed) wrote me: "Bodenheim was always asking for money, and from everyone. He had multiple excuses: his health, his teeth (or lack of them), a fictional friend who was on the point of committing suicide. . . . If you did not comply with his request, you were attacked for your meanness. If you did comply, you were insulted because of your affluence." From Franconia, New Hampshire, Robert Frost wrote Untermeyer that he "did well not to send the thankless Bodenheim to Europe. You have enough uses for your money taking mortgages on my next farm without patronizing poetry as she is written out of focus by the villain of the Village."[9]

Somehow, Minna borrowed enough to get them across the Atlantic. In England, Bodenheim lunched pleasantly several times with T. S. Eliot, stayed with Osbert Sitwell in Chelsea (they viewed each other as equally rare birds), and visited Wyndham Lewis. In a *Chicago Literary Times* article, "In Which the Assistant Editor Finds a Man Fully His Equal," Bodenheim wrote that, when he and Lewis parted, "we shook hands intensely, in the manner of two mock-antagonists who had discovered that their swords had been purchased from the same exclusive manufacturer." Conrad Aiken said that much fuss was made over Bodenheim, whom English writers such as Richard Aldington felt was the real Yankee stuff as opposed to the esoteric Aiken. But "the real thing" could not find the job he sought, and expenses were increased by the birth of the Bodenheim's only child, Solbert. Bodenheim also created some ill will by offering the unknowing Eliot, along with Aiken, as references for a lease. Mrs. Bodenheim again borrowed money—some from Blanche Guggenheim; and Aiken also contributed—and the family returned to New York City.

Life in America was economically as bad for them upon their arrival as it had been at the time they had departed. Louis Grudin observed that "his poverty and his physical distress were severe; beyond his hypochondria he fell ill a number of times (I visited him in a downtown hospital twice in one winter, I think); Minna and he still knocked about in the cheapest furnished rooms, except for a short while following their return from England with their baby, when they stayed with her parents in a tenement in the lower East Side slum." But, whether sick or wretched, he continued writing; and by 1923 he had written three more volumes of poetry and his first novel.

III Introducing Irony *(1922)*

Introducing Irony revealed a few slight shifts in Bodenheim's poetry, though irony exists in his published works from the start. He writes a number of poems answering his critics and he also includes more poems employing orthodox meter and rhyme. As though in compensation, he includes several poems dealing with esoteric characters, sights, and situations. He also presents familiar types: love poems to Minna and a collection of city poems.

"Impulsive Dialogue" is a fairly explicit colloquy between a poet and a critic. Originally, Bodenheim labeled his antagonists

"Poet" and "Undertaker," but in the *Selected Poems* he changes "Poet" to the more general "Traveller." The poem shows Bodenheim shakily defending his technique against a sensitive opposition. The critic's main objection to the poet's work is that it strains after originality only to "argue with its ghost," that it avoids "A simple beauty. . . ./ The sweeping purchase of an evening/ By an army of stars;/ The bold incoherence of love;/ The peaceful mountain-roads of friendship—/ These things evade your dexterous epigrams." The poet replies that poetic statement demands originality. Words, to strike the mind, must be used in strange new ways, even if—or because—this antagonizes the reader: "The words of most men kiss/ With satiated familiarity. . . ./ But one word in place of two/ Angers barmaids and critics."

Other poems dramatize Bodenheim's satiric attitudes toward poets and critics. In "Manners," he sports with those contemporaries who strike "The accepted lyrical note." These form a hypocritically polite and precious coterie captivated by their own moral posturing: "Gingerly the poets sit./ Gingerly they spend/ The adjectives of dribbling flatteries." A young girl enters their conclave, and secretly they study her body. They would publicly be shocked if she displayed any animal vitality: "Sirona, if you stood on your head/ Now, and waved the brave plan of your legs,/ Undisturbed by cloth," they would think her insane. They lack nerve in art and life: "Few men, Sirona, dare to become/ Completely vulgar, but many/ Nibble at the fringes."

In "Condensed Novel," Bodenheim wittily examines the essential life of Alvin Spar, avoiding "the abundant paragraphs/ With which a novelist interviews shades/ Of physical appearance in one man." Spar, who in his youth "Held half of the face that Aristotle/ May have had, and the pungent directness/ Of a stable-boy," marries only once, though many women love him. Bodenheim suggests his amorous career in sharp strokes, then adds: "The incidental people, chatter, and background?/ You will find them between/ Pages one and four hundred/ Of the latest bulk in prose." In "Simple Account of a Poet's Life" he sketches the biography of a writer, based upon himself, born in 1892 "When literature and art in America/ Presented a mildewed but decorous mien," and who dies in 1962 "with a grin at the fact/ That literature and art in America/ Were still presenting a mildewed, decorous mien." In these poems on literature, Bodenheim again asks for an art that is verbally imaginative, willing to take risks, that does not in ordinary fashion examine the surface texture of life, but that strikes in some fresh and uninhibited way at essentials.

The least effective poems of *Introducing Irony* are imaginative flights that, rather than soar into some empyrean of absolute truth, simply spin off nowhere near reality. Several of these begin with complex stage directions indicating that Bodenheim could not get everything into the poem that he wanted to. The directions also recall closet dramas that cumbersomely mix the ethereal and the all too solid: Shelley's *Prometheus Unbound* has a scene that opens with Ocean reclining close to shore. Bodenheim's "When Spirits Speak of Life" is prefaced by a paragraph explaining that three spirits are sitting on a low stone wall on top of a hill. After further explanation, the reader is told "the wall, the hill, and the figures exist only to the spirits who have created them."

"Emotional Monologue" similarly employs a paragraph setting the scene for an imaginary world Bodenheim presents: "A man is sitting within the enigmatic turmoil of a railroad station." Within the man "a monologue addresses an empty theatre." Beyond some tortured metaphors, the poem is easily understood, and, had it not been encumbered by its superstructure, it could have been one of the book's most interesting. The monologue travesties a stage performance and mocks the unrealities of real life. The poem's opening image, "I am strangling emotions/ And casting them into the seats/ Of an empty theatre" well evokes the empty, lonely, cynical man who delivers the monologue. Wit exists too in the drawing-out of the beginning conceit: "When my lifeless audience is complete,/ The ghosts of former emotions/ Will entertain their dead masters./ After each short act/ A humorous ghost will fly through the audience,/ Striking the limp hands into applause."

Another similarly elaborate poem, "Novel Conversations," begins in abstraction and ends in vagueness. Bodenheim's introduction states: "Certain favorite words of men have gathered in a vale made of sound-waves. These words, far removed from human tongues and impositions, enjoy an hour of freedom." The words who discuss life with one another in this brief poetic playlet are Emotion, Truth, Intellect, Art, Poetry, Fantasy, and Intellect. Emotion is the focal character and hero.

"Two Sonnets to My Wife" ("Two Sonnets to Minna" in the *Selected Poems*) show Bodenheim's continuing interest in the sonnet, which he ordinarily employs in character sketches. Using the conventional octave-sestet division and an *abbaabba/cdecde* rhyme, he achieves technical competence and regularity—if not the sparkle of Edna St. Vincent Millay. He hits upon some striking images, but an occasionally prosy flatness that is relatively unimportant in his longer, looser poems vitiates what must be a very tightly controlled form. For example, while the first two lines of Sonnet I are metaphorically interesting, the third seems almost a filler: "Because her voice is Schönberg in a dream/ In which harshness plays with lighter keys,/ This does not mean that it is void of ease."

Bodenheim's city poems continue his impressive biopsy of contemporary life. "Summer Evening: New York Subway Station" is representative in its free-verse depiction of the deadening effect urban life has upon cruelly defeated city dwellers. The poem also reveals Bodenheim's increasingly bitter presentation as his realism becomes less tender. The subway cars are "soiled caskets"; the people, "apathetic bales." As the cars jerk along, the poet sees a mosaic of underground life and the ersatz communication of two beaten dwellers. The first, a young girl, stands leaning against an iron girder, and is in effect part of the girder. As the subway car passes, her skirt rises (from the hot, dirty rush of displaced subway air), but she remains stationary, "A symbol of billowing torment. . . ./ Weariness has loosened her face/ With its shining cruelty." Bodenheim employs short, staccato lines to exhibit the dweller's pressured tension and to re-create the rhythm of consecutive pictures observed through windows of the speeding train. He describes random pieces of her clothing: "Her white cotton waist is a wet skin on her breast;/ Her black hat, crisp and delicate,/ Does not understand her head."

An old man stoops next to her, and he too is seen in quick impressions, "Sweat and wrinkles erupting/ Upon the blunt remains of his face." Harsh sounds echo the scene's cacophonous ugliness: "Perspiring violence derides/ The pathetic collapse of dirt. . . ./ Electric light is taut and dull. . . ./ Soiled caskets joined together/

Slide to rasping stand-stills." The fragmented and halting metaphors conclude with two simple lines set apart typographically from the rest of the poem, indicating the only sort of link between the defeated young and defeated old. These are seen as figures, not even as people: "Two figures on a subway platform,/ Pierced together by an old complaint."

Several city poems chronicle at greater length than "Summer Evening" the underdog or underworld characters. "The Scrubwoman" is a cold, detached analysis of what Bodenheim feels upon seeing a scrubwoman, rather than of what the woman might actually be. She is old and broken, clothed in the conventions of the day—"Neat nonsense, stamped with checks and stripes"—that rob her, for Bodenheim, of dignified poverty: "In other ages Time gave rags/ To hags without riches, but now he brings/ Cotton, calico, and muslin—/ Tokens of his admiration/ For broken backs." The lines reveal Bodenheim's growing concern for a beat whose rhythm meanders less and reflects meaning more. "Rags/ To hags without riches" breaks briefly into a loosely swinging measure, since Bodenheim wants to connote by tempo a certain attraction to aged poverty honestly bedecked in homespun. Then the alliterative "Cotton, calico, and muslin" with its two pauses slows down movement as each tawdry modern fabric is announced. Then the illusory reward of "Tokens of his admiration" is quickly undercut by the brief, brutal "For broken backs."

"Jack Rose" is an underworld story foreshadowing similar experiments in poetic narrative in *Bringing Jazz!* The poem is not syncopated, however; it employs iambic pentameter lines generally enjambed. Nearly all the rhymes are exact and masculine, and the poem speeds along briskly until its denouement, where the rhymes are still exact but each line is end-stopped. In this manner Bodenheim forces the reader to pause over the twist in the climax of his poetic short story. The poem's action concerns dope-peddling Jack Rose, who lapses into crime through self-doubt: "His vanity was small and could not call/ His egoism to the dubious hall/ Of fame where average artists spend their hour./ Doubting his powers he was forced to cower/ Within the shrill, damp alleys of his time." Jack, who sadistically enjoys watching the effects of his peddling, admires the arts "Of blundering destruction, like a monk/ Viewing a play that made him mildly drunk./ And so malicious and ascetic Jack/ Bent to his trade with a relentless back" until he meets May Bulger who smiled a "smile as smooth and hard as tile." May sells her body to Jack to buy dope for her brother, "to quiet a boy/ Who wept inanely for his favorite toy." Jack and May continue to hate each other until the brother dies. In a melodramatic ending entirely proper to this gangland pastoral, Jack plays at being amused by May's grief. May looks up at him and smiles, this time "A smile intensely stripped and subtly grim./ His hate felt overawed and in a trap,/ And suddenly his head fell to her lap./ For some time she sat stiffly in the chair,/ Then slowly raised her head and stroked his hair."

Bodenheim's attempt to invigorate poetry by this excursion into the New York underworld is not completely successful. The ending is sentimental; and, while it is proper to a tale picturing gangsters as does a cartoon, it detracts from impact of the climax. The verse is sometimes doggerel; but, treated as Bodenheim probably intended it, part tough-guy poetry, part parody of "gutsy" art, part "pop" art itself, the poem is an interesting experiment. The verse flows quickly, and Bodenheim wastes no words in setting scene or in portraying his crucial action. Jack and May, while not subtly analyzed, are types foreign to most poetry; and Bodenheim's attempt to enclose them in art is worthwhile. They are presented with a kind of honesty: he is a real crook and she is a real whore; and neither is particularly admirable. The story's conclusion shows them communicating with each other in other than a physical fashion. And neither is redeemed by the gesture, only humanized.

In "Pronounced Fantasy," Bodenheim works in the new jazz—specifically "blues"—idiom. The poem begins in an exotic Harlem locale: "A Negro girl with skin/ As black as a psychic threat,/ And plentiful swells of blonde hair,/ Sat at a badly tuned piano/ And vanquished her fingers upon the keys." Bodenheim then makes excellent use of "blues" lyrics—he is ahead of most of his contemporaries in doing so. In the *Selected Poems*, the Negro pianist sings "He brought me dresses and shoes./ He brought me diamonds and booze./ He brought me everything I could use/ But the jail-house key, that dog-gone jail-house key." The "key" of this "blues" song is both phallic and therefore that which liberates, and the literal key to the traditional "blues" jail. The singer's lament in the original 1922 version is less sexual but equally filled with remorse: "Wen' tuh Houston, tuh get mah trunk,/ Did'n get mah trunk, but ah got dam' drunk./ Well, ahm satisfi-i-ied/ Cause ah gotta be-e-e-ee." In the same version, the traditional "Railroad Blues" is effectively interpolated, helping to evoke the singer's sad plight. In both versions the mixture of exotic and "blues" imagery accomplishes a stylistic reflection of the Negress with blonde hair who spits "with religious incision/ At a parrot in a white spittoon."

Perhaps the most significant new direction in *Introducing Irony* is taken in "Seaweed from Mars." Bodenheim is able in this poem to portray a world of superior emotional existence in wildly fanciful, synesthetic images that are organic to his subject, since the visitor from Mars who relates the poem finds our language and senses hopelessly inadequate to explain life on his planet. What would be synesthesia on earth is simply a rough translation of sensuous life on Mars. Mars is an emotional alternative to conventional, mundane human existence, a world of essential intensity reached, one supposes, through escaping from what seems the crust of reality.

Bodenheim achieves in the poem his goal of avoiding surface reality and of removing into a deeper revelation of life where existence is different in kind and not merely in degree. This removal was a constant esthetic wish, for he deeply resented the dominant Realistic mode though he could successfully practice it. "Literary agencies want *realistic* work which I do not write," he said to his first wife in a letter. In the essay "Truth and Realism" he emphasized that "creative writing . . . is after all the ability to lie ferociously, delightfully, and with a canny fusion of under-and-overstatements that refuse to place an implicit faith in the flat daylight world of facts and averages."[10]

"Seaweed from Mars" is a monologue of well over two hundred lines in either the 1922 or 1946 version. Torban, a man from Mars, is the speaker. The work is one of Bodenheim's most technically ambitious, featuring various rhyme schemes—sometimes couplets, sometimes interlocking rhymes, sometimes occasional rhyme—and similarly varying metrical arrangements of usually four- or five-beat lines that often break into trochaic or iambic measure. Torban searches for images to explain the quality of life on Mars, clearly meant to be superior to earth. The images are frequently violent and extreme, both because of the differences between Mars and earth and because life on Mars swerves abruptly from one intense state to its polar opposite, according to season: "In Mars we have only two seasons,/ Spring and Autumn—their reasons/Rest in a treacherous sun/ That suddenly runs away." In autumn when "the trees have lost/ The diamond violence of Spring," the world of mind is intensely explored. Men "stand/ Still and deserted, while our minds/ Lunge into sweeping tensions/ Blending sound and form/ Into one search across the universe." Torban has difficulty explaining what this search discovers, since "All of your earthly words lurch/ Feebly upon the outskirts of my mind." But the quest results in a concept of the universe similar to that in Poe's "Eureka."[11] Physical shapes and sounds are only the shadows of ultimate essence. What one sees is only the trivial surface of reality: "Outward forms are but the graves/ Of sound, and all the different waves/ Of light and odor, they are sound/ That floats unshaped and loosely gowned./ When sound is broken into parts/ Your ears receive the smaller arts. . . ./ Your houses, hills, and flesh of red/ Are shapes of sound asleep or dead."

In the second season, spring, "Music, softer than the dins/ That rose from Autumn violins" (*din* would have been more correct) revives the mind. Spring is the season of intense physical communication in Mars, when "each man wins/ An understanding rest./ Once more we jest/ Upon the avenues, with voices/ One shade louder than the leaves and flowers,/ Or sail upon the coral seas/ And trade our words with molten ease." Other verses in chanted tetrameter explain that this ease and joy are strangely connected to sex: "We do not love and hate in Mars./ These earthly cries are flashing bars/ Of sound from which our minds are free. . . ./ For sex to us is but the ring/ Of different shades of thought in Spring." Earthlike sex is escaped not by elimination but by intensification, by purifying its communication: "Men recline upon the breast/ Of women in sheer, entering, grateful rest." (The 1922 version reads "Of women dissolving into thoughtful rest.") Life in Mars offers other paradoxes. In the 1922 version its intensity of existence is achieved through purged emotions:

"We have no emotions in Mars./ They are like long-healed wounds/ Whose scars are softened by the gleam of our minds." In the *Selected Poems* these lines are excised, perhaps because Bodenheim felt that the paradoxical achievement was not possible or not desired.

Bodenheim succeeds in "Seaweed from Mars" in making a difficult, abstruse position esthetically palatable. As philosophy, the investigation is not a serious, major contribution to American thought; but the consistently offbeat images well throw into relief the deadness and repression Bodenheim saw in America. His playing with rhyme, his alternation of an almost hypnotic, steady beat in some sections juxtaposed with the generally rapid, skimming movement of others, the rhythmical unloosening he achieves through enjambment—all make entertaining what could easily have been an amorphous, sticky piece of solemn foolishness.

Bodenheim is at his best in "Seaweed from Mars" and in the taut, tense, staccato lines of "An Acrobat, a Violinist, and a Chambermaid Celebrate," another successful poem. It does not deal with literal reality, as do his city poems, but with what he calls the "Geometry of souls." The poem satirizes man's "debris of words" in a world where "Nothing is wise except outline. . . ./ Men with few outlines in their minds/ Try to give the outlines dignity/ By moulding them into towers two inches high." Men should instead "scan your patterns/ For angles, oblongs, and squares of the soul." These outlines are apparently revealed through delicate, natural gestures which, despite their disparate origins, can merge and erase "the vague embellishment of flesh." Bodenheim examples this merging in the Cubist images he employs consistently throughout the poem: "While playing, the violinist's upper arm/ Bisected the middle of the acrobat's head/ As the latter knelt to hear,/ And the chambermaid/ Stretched straight on the floor,/ With her forehead/ Touching the tips of the violinist's feet." Thus the "geometry of the soul" can be seen or sensed. The poem itself attempts to discover this geometry by erasing the ordinary outlines of reality and by revealing what were to Bodenheim essential truths awaiting discovery and articulation.

IV Against This Age (1923)

Against This Age shows little change and no decline from Bodenheim's previous three volumes. The poems generally indict modern society as sordid and mean, but do so with little of the figurative tenderness of his earliest work. "New York City," in iambic pentameter couplets, contrasts the city's daytime ugliness with the dangerous beauty it achieves when masked by night. His impressions of bleak New York, its "undistinguished crates of stone/ And wood, the wounded dwarfs who walk alone—/ The chorus-girls whose indiscretions hang/ Between the scavengers of rouge and slang," are more effective than his depiction of what occurs when "The night, with black hands, gathers each mistake/ And strokes a mystic challenge from each ache./ The night, New York, sardonic and alert,/ Offers a soul to your reluctant dirt." The "black hands" of night are a cliché, and the image of stroking a "mystic challenge" from aches means less and less the more it is studied.

In "City Streets," a sonnet basically Italian but rhyming *abbacddc/efgefg,* Bodenheim combines two other old themes: the tendency toward escapism in much contemporary literature, and the deadening effect of urban life. Escapist literature is not necessary for the city dweller, he claims, for city life deadens even the desire for escape. The city crushes everything. The sestet claims "This is an age where flesh desires to shape/ Intense hyperboles in prose and verse,/ Transforming city streets and country lanes/ To backgrounds aiding physical escape./ But city streets are waiting to disperse/ With ruins the fight and plight of earthly pains."

The character sketches in *Against This Age* focus on city lives made small and dirty. Bodenheim writes without much sympathy for the underdog and without recognizing any positive evil to combat. His sketches show almost no politically radical criticism. "Poem to a Policeman," for example, begins describing a "Marionette-fanatic" wielding his "active club" during a riot. Ordinarily this sort of scene, in *New Masses* poetry or in much fiction of the period—Dos Passos' perhaps—would provide the opportunity for bitter onslaught against the forces of authority who oppress the worker. But Bodenheim uses it to engage in a discussion of life after death and the possibility of reincarnation. The policeman is not even treated as a social evil. "Intimate Scene" takes place in a bedroom that has earned its "sympathy of dirt," where "Many contorters of bellies/ Have stirred an urgent travesty/Shielded by your greasy dusk." In the bedroom a man and woman bicker and have sex without much pleasure. "Highly Deliberate Poem" tells about a small-time entertainer with "the face of a spell-bound, hairless rat." The singer is momentarily shaken by the fear of death, but he is too insignificant for Death to bother with: "Death, who has listened with fastidious ennui, strolls off to slay/ A Negro infant newly born."

These last three poems reveal no prosodic advancement in Bodenheim's free verse. He favors a short three- or four-beat line usually, with frequent enjambment. He almost never comes to a full periodic pause within the line. While his earlier free-verse lines often terminated at some natural speech pause, the lines of these poems are frequently concluded arbitrarily by syntactic unit. He will, for example, end one line with a noun and begin the next with a prepositional phrase. In "Dogma Visits the Country-Side" he does this: "His legs divide the spacious tragedy/ Of distance into small translation/ Of steps. . . . /Bearing the trans-figured skirmish/ Of spiritual moods that men call color." He also breaks his lines sometimes in the middle of phrasal units, as in "Highly Deliberate Poem": "At sixty the rat will be a gorged/ Machiavelli, wondering/ Whether or not he has blundered." Here the lineation is for emphasis, to increase the surprise value of "Machiavelli." Often, however, the lines are simply divided by rhythmic length after four or at most five beats; and no consistent pattern of division emerges.

One of the few poems in *Against This Age* showing development of interest is "Regarding an American Village,"—Bodenheim's first full-scale employment of American small-town life. In the tradition of Masters' *Spoon River Anthology*, Sherwood Anderson's prose *Winesburg, Ohio*, and Edwin Arlington Robinson's "Tilbury Town" poems, the work presents character vignettes of village life. The poem is possibly the immediate result of Bodenheim's friendship at the MacDowell Colony with Robinson, whom he admired. The first section of Bodenheim's poem states that he will follow a middle course in his portrayals: "I have not contempt or praise/ To give you—no desire/ To rip off, discovering/ Skin, and undulations known as sin,/ And no desire to revise you/ With glamorous endearments of rhyme."

He then depicts lives of small cowardice and frustration. First is Jacob Higgins, "Belated minstrel—sings and dances/ On the edge of the cliff./ Once fiendish and accurate,/ His greed has now become unskillful,/ Visualizing Death as a new/ Mistress who must be received with lighter manners." Jacob buys his grandchild "five cents wuth [*sic*] of candy" to expiate his greed. Cliff-dancing now only in his mind, he cackles in his chair next to the stove. Another old man "like a blurred/ Report of winter, seizes/ The firmer meaning of a joke/ About the Ree-publican parteee." Elsewhere in the store, Bob Wentworth, bowed by forty years of town life, lives vicariously as he "separates the mail/ With the guise of one intent/ On guessing the contents of a novel." Agnes Holliday picks up one letter from her secret, distant lover, and thinks "reproachfully" of her empty bed; then she quickly remembers "Oh, she had forgotten:/ Sugar, corn, and loaves of bread." When a skittish boy asks her to the weekly dance at the next town, she weighs "concrete pleasures" against "puny, fruitless dreams." The portraits conclude with nightfall, when all "crave the narcotic safety of home." Bodenheim restrains his rhapsodic tendencies in the poem and presents his portraits with relative simplicity. The diction is unforced and appropriate to a description of small-town life and characters. The quiet wit displayed is also appropriate to the wintry New England village he recaptures. He shows in this work the kind of seemingly uncomplicated poetry he could write so well. His accomplishment in the poem is not great but definite.

V The Sardonic Arm (1923)

The poems in Bodenheim's second book of 1923, *The Sardonic Arm*, are less sharp in outline than those in *Against This Age;* they are some of his most suggestive and some of his most diffuse verse. In the series "Portraits," his images sometimes blur what are really simple statements: in "Stenographer" the secretary's superiority over the "droning man beside her" is announced by the lines "Intellect,/ You are an electrical conspiracy/ Between the advance guards of soul and mind"; a shop girl's beauty in "Shop Girl" becomes metaphysically significant—"Yellow roses in your black hair/ Hold the significance/ Of stifled mystics defying time."

The "Captain Simmons" poems, including "More About Captain Simmons" and "Captain Simmons' Wife," similarly display a lack of precise characterization and a greater reliance upon suggestive, unsensuous images, at least compared to the portraits in "Regarding an American Village" and in "Highly Deliberate Poem." One learns that Simmons is old, "With a body like the fading dream/ Of an athlete, and a face/ Made womanly by age"; but one never learns why he is a captain or what kind of a captain he is. Probably "Captain" is a title generally signifying some authoritarian figure, and is therefore to be attacked. Simmons' intellect has apparently stifled his emotions: one learns this through a series of overwrought images reminiscent of the house-mind allegory Bodenheim used in "Old Age": "An arbitrary architect/ Became his mind, and planned/ Cathedrals, mansions, and shops/ In a room enclosed by hair./ And so a crowded town/ Occupied the dwarfed miles in his head." This crowding breeds slum conditions, which in turn force some buildings "into the realm of emotion." Only half-breeds live there. Yet Simmons is never able—and in old age he increasingly recognizes this—to inhibit his emotional self completely: "Captain Simmons' black suit/ Fitted him loosely while his mind/ Became him tightly."

Simmons' wife has a more orderly mind that has "attained/ A weak and exquisite indirectness." She moves "in a calculating trot,/ Relinquishing hairsbreadths of her life/ With each step, and gathering/ Atoms of humour and melancholy/ Into one last excuse for existence." She has kept control of herself as her husband has not, yet her description concludes with an image hinting she might have liked living otherwise: "Again, she scanned the spots/ On a bridal-gown and planned,/ As she had done for years,/ To send it to an imaginary cleaner."

The imagery in the Captain Simmons poems demonstrates Bodenheim's unvisual metaphoric language, which is generally of two varieties. First is the image that one is only to graze and clearly not to visualize, for the picture would then be cluttered and ludicrous. Captain Simmons' head filled with mansions and shops is obviously not to be imagined literally. Bodenheim's point is that Simmons' intellect is as unhealthily crowded as the city, but the picture is nonetheless literally there. The city metaphor is so fully developed that only with difficulty can one prevent seeing a man's head split, as in a headache advertisement, to reveal trip-hammered streets inside. The second kind of unvisual image is shown in the six lines beginning "She moved in a calculating trot." Here, one understands the image less, the more one investigates its elusive literal implications. But the general shape of the metaphoric pattern is recognizable. The suggestion of a woman comically bustling through life and sadly, regretfully aging is strong.

Of course much of the book's imagery is immediately connotative. Literary theories are attacked in lucid figures. "Realism" mocks those who insist upon that mode, and those who, perhaps like Sherwood Anderson, find great spiritual significance in rural meandering. A farm is just a place where "Horses, pigs, and cows/ Assemble their discontent./ The result is Chinese Orchestra." The animals do not even realize that their voices should portray the farmer in his house, "The hackneyed prose of his life;/ The expanding soul of his corn-fields." Instead, the farmer "stands, a figure of niggardly order. . . ./ His grey beard is the end of a rope/ That has gradually throttled his face." And so much for the farm mystique.

The city is imaged as even more explicitly mordant than in earlier poems in "North Clark Street, Chicago." A companion to "South State Street: Chicago," the poem begins as did the earlier work with a picture of the surrounding buildings. But where before "Rows of blankly box-like buildings/ Raise[d] their sodden architecture/ Into the poised lyric of the sky," now "Tame and ghastly coffins/ Display their shamefaced greys and reds/ Against the passive vividness of morning." No illusion of hope exists now, no dreamed of place of escape." Afternoon has fallen on this street,/ Like an imbecilic organ-grinder/ Grinning over his discords." To this hideous music "Dead men and women spin/ Their miracles of motion/ Upon the greyness of this street."

Bodenheim's antipathy to critics is also well imaged in another Torban poem called "Fantasy," in which a number of concrete images depict the abstract ideal of what Bodenheim considered contemporary criticism: a "Cabaret in which Malice,/ Dignified or torrential,/ Turns creators into beetles/ And slays them ingeniously;/ Cabaret in which Erudition,/ Tempted by emotional coquettes,/ Swaggers greyly past the footlights;/ Cabaret in which lust/ Defends itself with thoughtful monologues."

Just as *The Sardonic Arm* continues the earlier style of Bodenheim's images and repeats his standard themes, it displays no real prosodic experimentation. Few poems are rhymed, and few feature manipulation of line length or meter in any consistent, meaningful fashion. Bodenheim's free verse of the period is often structurally similar to the patterns of newspaper headlines, but this resemblance may not be planned. Such lines as those introducing "Woman" do, however, resemble a page-one head:

> They worship musical sound
> Protecting the breast of emotion.
> Their feelings pose as fortune-tellers. . . .

The short, relatively even, and journalistically direct rhythm contrasts with the highly unjournalistic diction Bodenheim ordinarily employs; and it provides an ironic framework for his ideas.

The volume does contain, if nothing technically new, a few poems that reaffirm old ideas in a fresh way. In at least three poems, Bodenheim investigates the interplay of essence and shadow, the meaning that impersonal object and death impart to life: he discusses what is real and what is not, what is the real significance of seeming unreality.

The first of these poems is frankly entitled "Platonic Narrative." Bodenheim begins his investigation with the line "Tomato soup at four A.M.," which parodies Wallace Stevens' "Disillusionment of Ten O'Clock" (published in book form the same year in *Harmonium*). Then he describes two lovers who become, through love, "the essences of Plato," or rather who strive to become those essences: knees "With their prominence of bone" commit "treason to our souls." The lovers' attempt partly succeeds, however: "Our backs against the cushions/ Had disappeared, and we did not move/ For fear that all of us/ Might rush away through the openings" that presumably have released essence. After a time, the two return from their ecstatic heights to drink the soup, which has now become "an insipid fluid." They are now superior to the world of material objects about them, since they give the floor, for example, "a reason for existence," and permit laughter to "Peer . . . through the crevices of our eyes," traditionally mirrors or revealers of the soul.

In "Platonic Narrative" meaning is imparted life by the ecstatic, released lovers; in "Time, Infinity, and Eternity Descend Upon a Black Hat," a simple black derby hat is more meaningful than the life it caps. Like Stevens' jar in "Anecdote of the Jar" (also published in *Harmonium*), the hat orders the world that surrounds and is under it: "The black derby hat,/ Poised and incorruptible,/ Curves its black 'no' to the senses." To the superficial observer, "The black derby hat is only a sugar-bowl/ Turned upside-down and out of place. . . ./ Or a symbol of bulky manhood/ Swaggering in an ancient trap." But, to more penetrating eyes, the hat represents essential, shaping substance in an enormous and blind universe, "defending its realm/ Against the pompous indifference/ Of Time, Infinity, and Eternity." The hat has, in fact, a sharp reality denied its wearer: "The black derby hat is an outline of earth,/ Bold and abrupt. . . ./ And he who wears it is only a helpful accident/ Bringing publicity to the hat." A spot of meaning in a world of urban chaos, the hat's life is charmed and free: "And so, the black derby hat,/ Gliding through the frantic defeats/ Of a city street,/ Coolly protects its realm/ Against the scarecrow contempt/ Of Time, Infinity, and Eternity." The hat controls, gives order to, "protects its realm." It defines reality by its existence.

Death defines life in a thematically related poem, "Dear Minna I": "Death, you take the stiffly obvious shapes/ Of objects and crack them with your fingers. . . ./ And I am grateful to you for that." The death of a shopowner frees him, "Robs him of microscopical convictions." The owner's death is paralleled by the breaking of his bric-a-brac: the "cups, jars, and vases" are now pieces. Once merely "symmetrical and empty,/ And immersed in the task of holding nothing,/ Now they have snatched a voice from fragments;/ Spell many an accidental sentence;/ Renounce the hollow lie." Order is here brought about by seeming disorder, just as death adds meaning to life by destroying smallness and ignobility. Essence of soul, the black hat, and death give meaning to life and are interrelated. Black is, of course, the color of death; and essence and death are liberations from the body.

Mention of Wallace Stevens in connection with two of these poems reintroduces the topic of influences upon Bodenheim. While certain pervasive sources of the time not doubt reached him in a general way, or were manifested temporarily in individual passages, he seems to have had no contemporary models, no specific teachers, for the poetry he wrote. Bodenheim never associated himself with any so-called school of modern poetry, and he usually criticized such coteries that existed. Since he was almost pathologically anti-authoritarian, he could not consciously subject his art to the discipline of studying others; and he was recognized by his contemporaries, Pound and Aiken, for example, as a renegade or solitary.

But no artist is completely isolated from his time, and none springs full grown. Certain elements in his verse were common to contemporary poetry. He wrote, for example, a number of pseudo-Chinese poems similar to those of Pound, Amy Lowell, or Allen Upward. In mixing the abstract with the concrete, employing consciously repugnant or strange imagery, oxymoron and synesthesia, Bodenheim reflects the so pervasive influence during the post-World War I years of the French Symbolists. But he writes poetry using these techniques before Symbolism becomes of heavy general influence upon American poetry. It is plausible that he learned more from the peripherally Symbolistic English and American poets such as Swinburne and Poe, for Bodenheim had no formal academic training in poetry and did not know French. Arthur Symons' *The Symbolist Movement in Literature* (rev. ed., 1919) was of course available to him.

Bodenheim mentions Baudelaire in "A Poet's Story" (in *Seven Poets in Search of an Answer* [1944]) as closing ranks with Whitman and Plato to form the vanguard of his new poetry, but Baudelaire's work differs essentially from Bodenheim's, in which no true dandyism or satanism exists. Baudelaire's definition of beauty as "quelque chose d'ardent et de triste, quelque chose d'un vague, laissant carrière à la conjecture. . . . Le mystère, le regret sont aussi des caractères du Beau" could also be the concept of beauty exemplified in some of Bodenheim's poems; but, if Bodenheim needed the concept taught, Poe could have done the job as well. And Bodenheim lacks the insistence upon formal poetic patterns so obvious in Poe, Baudelaire, or the more imagistically amorphous Mallarmé.

In *L'Influence du Symbolisme Français sur La Poésie Americaine*, René Taupin discusses Bodenheim's Symbolist inheritance, and he concludes that Bodenheim has mastered only the tricks of the Symbolists.[12] Taupin is fooled by some slight praise Bodenheim gave the Symbolists in an essay for the *New Republic* that he quotes, by some scattered remarks of Bodenheim minimizing emotion in poetry—but he was writing of others' emotions, the readers' mostly, and of the poet's emotions baldly stated and not imaged—and by Bodenheim's use of "l'ironie, le sarcasme et d'autres objets secondaires que Laforgue et d'autres poètes de sa force employaient." So Taupin finds that Bodenheim employs Symbolistic decoration only, and that behind the decoration is "banalité sans importance . . . jamais le symbole comme le comprenait Mallarmé, jamais l'image comme la comprennent le imagistes, mais le pavoisement, la parade, le décor sans acteur, et tout cela avec une richesse d'accessoires qui vient du depouillement."

Taupin is wrong, not because he finds Bodenheim inferior to Mallarmé, but because he examines Bodenheim as though he were a Symbolist poet, which he is not. For Bodenheim the decoration was the poem, in part anyway. The turns of phrase in each individual work, the coupling of words in a fresh manner, were important. Metaphoric equivalents for emotions were also important. Structure was not so important. Interlocking and complex images relating to fairly consistent sets of philosophic attitudes are almost completely absent in Bodenheim's work. He had ideas, of course, but these were suggested often quite directly, if not clearly, in the so-called decoration of his individual poems. To examine Bodenheim's poems as Symbolist documents is to examine two specifically unparallel bodies of literature.

Bodenheim read English and American poets too. He read and praised Keats, Coleridge, Tennyson, Swinburne, and the Americans Poe, Whitman, and Crane. He does not seem to have read with enough interest to mention the seventeenth-century metaphysicals such as Donne and Marvell, who were so popular with his contemporaries. Some of Bodenheim's poems resemble Stephen Crane's, whose "The Newspaper," for example, displays the same seemingly loose free verse, the same mixture of levels of diction, the same tendency to define, and even some of the same attitudes (a newspaper concentrates "eternal stupidities") that one finds in Bodenheim's work. The sardonic stance and image pervades the poetry of both.

[73]

But the premium Bodenheim placed on originality, on the idiosyncratic style, as well as his psychological inability to subject himself to the discipline of others, in poetry or in daily life, limit any definite and intense influence upon his art. He imaged art in "Esthetics, Criticism, and Life" as a child wailing in rebellion against his parents. Nor did he ever violently shuck off one style in favor of another. While he refined his talent, and while his later radical poetry demanded a shift in some attitudes, he did not proceed through radically different stages as did Pound or Yeats. Bodenheim's metamorphoses, to judge from *Blackguard*, occurred before he began publishing. For good or bad, his school was his own.

VI Blackguard (1923)

Bodenheim's autobiographical first novel, *Blackguard*, showed the growth of a young poet in lower-middle-class Chicago, and presents him as an esthete and a miscreant. While not the best-fashioned of Bodenheim's books, it displays a comic self-portrait and a nostalgic pathos rare in the usually bitter writer: tonally, the work is similar to O'Neill's *Ah Wilderness*. The book's defects were repeated in his novels throughout Bodenheim's career: authorial intrusions, shaky handling of point of view (often a talky omniscience), lack of focus, and sometimes subservience to irrelevant matter. At their worst, Bodenheim's novels seem tracts designed for revenge.

Examples of Bodenheim's characteristic obtrusions are numerous in *Blackguard*. When his hero, Carl Felman, walks down a Chicago street observing children's games, Bodenheim comments that the play masks feelings created by summer's "sensual madness"; and he adds: "most people are incapable of actual thought, and thinking to them is merely emotion that calmly plots for more concrete rewards and visions." Another repeated fault in Bodenheim's fiction is his penchant for artily self-conscious dialogue or reverie. "The shadows gave your face," young Carl's girlfriend says, "a soft excuse, and you looked half like a sprite and half like a martyr. There was an indelicately impish weariness on your face." And the young woman is not being satirized.

But Bodenheim's novelistic defects should not obscure his

accomplishments. His fiction offers keen social analysis and some-times powerful investigations of contemporary urban life and of mainly disaffected urban types. In *Blackguard* he employs one of the central myths of American fiction: a youth's education in the city. Beginning with Charles Brockden Brown's *Arthur Mervyn* and continuing through J. D. Salinger's *The Catcher in the Rye* and Ralph Ellison's *Invisible Man* and beyond, the city has provided urban landscapes dangerous as the wilderness to test the sensitive young man. The American quest is a city quest: a major theme of much native fiction and of *Blackguard;* for the city is the dominant force in young Carl Felman's growing up.

Bodenheim fuses the myth of the city quest with the career of a now-familiar American city type, the marginal Jew. Carl Felman must combat two enemies, the cold, brutalizing city and what he considers a crumbling tradition. Combined with the story of a poet's growth, the themes produce a touching, comic portrait of the silly, dedicated artist who collides with the husk of a devitalized establishment.

The novel opens with Carl returning home to Chicago after several years in the army and bumming around. He is twenty-one, and for the first time he realizes the city's brute impersonality. A crowd of people is really "many isolations joined to a huge one." Office buildings are "coffins standing on end." His parents' apartment fits in one of many similar rows "standing like factory boxes awaiting shipment, but never called for." Like a returning prodigal, he evades the neighbors by climbing into his parents' apartment through a side window. His mother has always yelled at Carl's father for leaving it open: a thief might come in, she claims. Throughout the book Carl sees himself as a criminal and actually reveals a talent for petty thievery. Whatever are the glories of Carl's freedom, innocence is not one.

The apartment's tawdriness reflects the sterility of traditionless city life and the family's thinness of Jewish culture. Carl sees that the room has not changed in his absence; it still contains "the modest and orderly showing of cut-glass and silverware—tinsel of an old defeat; the plaster of paris bust of an Indian, violently colored and bearing an artificial scowl." Displaying a polyglot of pseudo-culture, the room jumbles together the Indian; a washed-out, pink-and-blue effigy of a courtier; and a brass clock "moulded into crude cherubs interwined with stiff blossoms." Carl, who slumps into a chair in one corner of the ugly, cluttered, uncohesive room that symbolizes his family life, shouts: "Damn it, I'll get out of this some day." Then he automatically takes a soiled bit of paper from his pocket and with sensual satisfaction goes over one of his poems. Thus both the enemy—the city, his class, his family —and the mode of attack or escape—his art—are effectively described.

Carl's parents bear the force of his attacks. While they love the young man, both are able to propose only ways of life completely antipathetic to their son. And both place a painful burden on Carl when they imagine him a spindly avatar of their own now-blasted dreams. Together they are "middle-aged Jews with starved imaginations and an anger at the respectable poverty of their lives." The mother is a woman whose emotions are "garrulously bitter because of the material strait jackets in which they had writhed for years." Like Bodenheim's own mother, she comes from a wealthy and respected family. Felman's father hovers on the rim of absolute failure, tottering but never quite plunging. Both want Carl to stop taking poetry seriously—it is no profession for an adult—and to "go out and get a regular job, like other men." Carl's mother even buys him a new suit in which to job hunt.

But Carl fails to get work at the factories where he applies because his clothes are too new. "Factories he goes to!" Mrs. Felman cries in a voice like a rattled skillet. "I bought him a new suit and shoes this morning so he could look for common dirty work! It's terrible. Here we sent him to high school for four years and his only ambition is to work as a common laborer." Mrs. Felman's strictures provide a semi-comic chorus to Carl's self-conscious attempts at liberation through poetry. Her Jewish mother's wisdom is expressed again and again on the same themes: *Martyrdom*: "You're a big boy now, yes, a big boy, and you know that we've sacrificed everything to give you a good education . . . not that we regret it, no indeed." *Education*: College only "fills your head, you know, with a lot of nonsense." *Art*: "Writing is no business for a strong, sensible boy." *Financial success*: "Mrs. Feinsthal was telling me at my whist-club today that her son Harry is making piles of money with Leibman and Company." *Success in art*: "Mrs. Bodenheim was telling me she has a cousin who writes love stories for the *Daily Gazette*. Nice stories that make you laugh and cry. And this girl gets twenty dollars apiece for them, too."

Carl's father usually seconds his wife, though he is also the first to relent in any argument. But under the mother's friendly advice runs a current of bitterness: her hate is partly against the son, but more directly against the father. Bodenheim focuses so much on Carl's point of view that conflicts between the parents are more implied than described, but the conflict clearly exists. The mother's main objection against Carl is not so much that he is in danger of becoming a poet, for that is incomprehensible, but that he seems to be following his father's pattern of failure. This attitude is shown in one of the book's most honest and powerful scenes when Carl is fired from his job as telephone lineman and precipitates a family squabble. At first, only mild recriminations are uttered; but then Carl's father tells him not to be a "poor schlemiel" all his life. Carl angrily throws his father's own failure at him, reminding him that twenty years of work as traveling salesman and of running a general store have brought him neither money nor happiness. "You recommend a treacherous wine," Carl says; "I've inherited nothing from you save your curious inability at making money."

The shamed and tormented father sits silently for a moment and gazes with unreading eyes at the newspaper. Then he blurts "Yes, I've been too kind-hearted for my own good, dammit, but I want that you should be different. It's been too easy for people to swindle me. Yes, I want you to show them something that your poor old father couldn't. Yes." By now, the mother's attack has switched to the father; for her rage at her husband's failure can no longer be controlled. "We would have our nice store this very minute if your father had listened to me," she says mournfully. "He never would let me handle the reins. I knew how to be firm with people, believe me, but your father. . . ." And on her bitterness spills. "All your wildness, Carl, has come from your father's side and not mine."

Mr. Felman and Carl smile at each other, and Carl for the first time feels on the verge of a slight communion with the tired old man. But the moment passes as the argument sputters on. Several pages later Carl enters the world of Chicago poetry, and the novel returns only fleetingly to the family situation. After the trauma of

Carl's sweetheart's death, he and his father confront each other
for the last time as a child and parent. Carl's rebirth following the
trauma—rebirth in that he finally cuts himself off from his Jewish
lower-middle-class heritage, and stops writing poetry as merely
an escape mechanism—is ritualized by his shedding blood in fighting his father.

The first half of the novel, that dealing with the city-family
struggles, is the best partly because of its comic objectivity. Carl
postures before his incredulous parents—"I have tried to save a
possible poet from death," he explains about his return; "but it
seems that his skin must burn. I've come back now to make his
coffin and stud it with gold"—his Jewish mother simply replies:
"I'll get you something from the ice-box." He tries to rush his sensitive soul quickly by the doorstoop crones and must endure
"Mo, this is Mister Felman, who's just back from the army." He
scans impossible "want-ads": "Wanted—young man for clerical
work; must be neat, industrious, wide-awake, sober, well educated, reliable, good at details, ambitious, honest, painstaking;
salary, twelve dollars."

Told to clean up before the financially successful star boarder
enters, he feels "like an ignoble marionette who was being hastily
mended behind the curtain for fear that he might cast ridicule
upon the sleekly vacant play." The city dwellers Carl meets are
appropriately animalistic or tense mechanisms: he sees a pick-
pocket "with the face of a shaved fox" and later hears a woman
whose "voice snapped like a succession of breaking wires." One
girl with whom he has a touching yet one-sided love affair—he can
offer her only his childlike desire to be loved—significantly loves
him without comprehending him: "I adore you when you say
things that I can't understand," she says.

Once Felman begins emerging as a young poet and mixes with
the Chicago intelligentsia, the book loses much freshness and
charm.[13] His posturing is now meant to be taken seriously; and,
as a serious figure, he is too often only fatuous. One of the crucial
events of this part of the book, Carl's love affair with "Olga Rame-
ly," is described in grotesquely coy terms. Olga's eyes "seemed
to be two drops of quivering sweat left behind by an emotional
crucifixion. They were sensitive with essences." Instead of feeling
sadness at Olga's demise, the reader's strongest emotion is apt to

be relief. And Carl's growth as a poet is not convincing. One learns that from writing flowery, imitative verses he begins to seek truth through poetry; but his supposed artistic development is unaccompanied by any increased awareness or perception. Carl seems much the same person at the book's conclusion as at its start: he experiences no growth in wisdom, only additional rebellion.

Carl does achieve peace, if not knowledge, after his storm and stress. With Olga's death, Carl leaves home after his farewell fight. He travels to Memphis where he lives with his uncle, Dr. Max Edleman. Treated with some questioning but with respect, Carl finally determines to live as a poet—to the world as a "blackguard." He still sees poetry as an anti-social act, and himself as an offender: the younger Carl thought himself "a huge black criminal staggering beneath the weight of unreleased plots." At the very end of the book he joins with another of life's honest rejects, the prostitute Georgie May. They agree to "live together without touching each other and each . . . will be the monk and nun that he should have been." Hand in hand they stagily traipse away— Bodenheim nearly always had trouble ending his novels—to neither knows what, "a noble rascal and an ascetic prostitute."

Bodenheim later wrote better novels, but he never again displayed so much raw autobiographical material. He learned to pay more attention to the matter and manner of his work, less to his own personal philosophy. He learned to pare peripheral comment and action from the urban themes he dealt with and to limit purely personal revelation. But he never again captured the sad and bitter comedy of youth as he did in *Blackguard.*

VII Crazy Man (1924)

Bodenheim's next novel, *Crazy Man,* constitutes a considerable advancement over *Blackguard* in that it is less uneven and less awkward technically. Its action is divided into three parts: in the first, the life of Selma Thallinger is described in all its drab meaninglessness until she meets the crazy man John Carley. In the second, Carley's life is described; his slow development as a Christ-Robin Hood is depicted to the time when he is brutally beaten at the dance hall where Selma works. The third section shows the effect of the two on each other: Carley's strange Christ-like example initiates Selma into a meaningful existence, and Carley gains his first female disciple.

Selma is curiously unaffected by the surface immorality of her life. Like Dreiser's Sister Carrie and Jennie Gerhardt, she has an essentially uncorruptible innocence, and a moral solidity or impenetrability that enables her to maintain a kind of peace despite the occasional turbulence of her life on the fringes of nighttown. Selma's innocence stems partly from her moral insensitivity, for the reader is told "it is impossible to corrupt something that is not prepared to receive the wisdom of decay, and some natures remain unmarked because they do not receive the polluting pain which is understanding." Yet her obtuseness is not completely intellectual; it is more a failure to admit the moral strictures of a corrosive, restraining society. This moral apartness endows her with "an honest serenity . . . a peace she could fall back on in times of need," but it has also insulated Selma from achieving satisfaction from the life she has determined to lead. She recognizes that the life about her offers no true fulfillment and constantly rebels from accepting the patterns she observes in her environment. But she can formulate no alternatives to these patterns: she can only react, not act. Before Carley arrives, her rebellion is conventional, and she remains unaroused, "a somnambulist simulating passion." She mocks "the forces that would seek to lower her," but she barely comprehends them and knows no others.

Selma's existence is narrowly circumscribed by her family and by the dime-a-dance joint where she works nights. Her family is lower middle class, ill-educated, materialistic, and sexually hypocritical. Neither the father nor mother exerts more than superficial authority over Selma, and she attempts to remain aloof from their threatened and sometimes actual inroads upon her freedom. She lacks the drive or independence to leave them to live her own life. Mrs. Thallinger—fat, homely, slovenly—criticizes Selma's free behavior around the house: "Se-elma, what do you mean by layin' here stark naked. . . . Ain't you got no shame?" Selma's father—a crippled pool-hall loiterer, a beaten, ineffective man—stays with his wife neither from loyalty nor love, but "because she had become a habit whose departure would have threatened the orderly structure of life." Brother Jo, a minor tough, sees the city as a jungle where real men seduce the sisters and wives of others to show their own powers of conquest.

Rebelling from her empty home life, Selma turns to the demi-world of the ironically named "Merry Grotto," a depressingly bleak and tawdry dance hall where the girls dance "like painted, flexible, unemotional dolls." The Merry Grotto offers no more freedom than the home—and no more joy; for action is habitual and hypocritical in both places. At home, one feigns innocence; at the hall, mild lust. In Selma's lower west-side neighborhood a dead, defeated sameness dominates the "prostrate slab of stone" that is each identical building. The Merry Grotto offers little more of life with its circumscribing wall panels of—further irony for city dwellers—"sylvan scenes," its electric light clusters covered with red cheesecloth, and its squawking third-rate orchestra. Life in each place is symptomatic of city life: people are crowded together in false intimacy; and this physical closeness demands a frantically assembled mask to keep one's self from the enemy so near.

Even though the Merry Grotto seems liberated from official morality, it brings little satisfaction to its inhabitants, and is really just another part of the brutalized and cheapened urban civilization. Sex becomes a means of asserting physical superiority, of proving desirability; but it is otherwise joyless: "You gave yourself at irregular intervals because this indicated that you were not a back number, and that your physical characteristics were . . . prized by men."

Vaguely "oppressed by the sense that something wasn't right," Selma drifts coldly and essentially untouched through the only world of action she knows. Her behavior is only habitual: "Selma spoke without indignation, as though she were supplying the proper sounds to a familiar sense of disgust." Trained by the society she hates, she cannot alone transcend that society; and she clearly suggests the trapped creature John Dewey and James Tufts described in *Ethics*.[14]

The freedom of an agent who is merely released from direct external obstructions is formal and empty. If he is without resources of personal skill, without control of the tools of achievement, he must inevitably lend himself to carrying out the directions and ideas of others. If he has not powers of deliberation and invention, he must pick up his ideas casually and superficially from the suggestions of his environment and appropriate the notions which the interests of some class insinuate into his mind. If he have not powers of intelligent self-control, he will be in bondage to appetite, enslaved to routine, imprisoned within the monotonous round of imagery flowing from illiberal interests, broken only by wild forays into the illicit.

The outside agent saving Selma from habitual and petty rebellion is John Carley,[15] a rebel who consciously seeks to shock society into victimizing him. Carley steps into Selma's life at the height of his powers, with years of rigorous testing behind him. Affecting a simple, Whitmanesque costume–"clean, rough clothes, with a dark blue, workingman's shirt open at the throat"–he courts personal destruction to spread his doctrine of charity, freedom, and mutual understanding. His good is "the good that comes from trying to understand the people around you, and . . . evil . . . the evil that comes from closing your eyes to what's in front of you." Carley had been for most of his life a male counterpart to Selma: he has been oppressed by the same hypocritical society and educated for the same materialistic, habitual, grind. He is, however, more intelligent than Selma. In order to get enough money to attract the women he desired, he became a thief. He was dissatisfied with that life, though he could, like Selma, envision no other. While known as "Educated Johnny" for his habit of reading a book to "cool off" after brawling, Carley is not always smart enough to elude the police. Much of his life has been spent in prison. Through reading in jail (earlier he had stolen necessary books) such authors as "Havelock Ellis, Stirner, Bergson, Nietzsche, Shaw, Schopenhauer, Spinoza, Dostoevski, Anatole France, Flaubert, Browning, Verlaine" (oh brave new prison library), he slowly begins constructing his own philosophy. He experiences a conversion–to his own religion–and finally realizes why he had become a thief: "In this transfiguration Christ adopted the garments of a thief, but they bore the appearance of a deliberate and necessary masquerade. He wore them as part of His journey to a second crucifixion and with them he was inviting the world to nail Him in a novel fashion."

While Carley's religion contains a Christ, it admits no opposing forces of darkness; it contends that sin does not exist as a theological vice: "Never mind all this junk about Heaven, and Hell, and the Devil, and sin. Particularly sin. That was made up to frighten people into acting decent toward each other." Carley defines sin in terms that John Steinbeck's later hero Jim Casey in *The Grapes of Wrath* would agree to: "There's only one sin . . . and that's if one person gets ugly with his hands and tries to make the other person do something the other person doesn't want to do," and "no one is ever ashamed unless he's doing something that part of him doesn't want to do."

Employing Christ as a historical model, Carley rejects both His teachings and Christianity. "Christ made two mistakes," he says. "He didn't see that men and women can't stop their natural desires by stamping all over them." The second mistake is that "He told people to believe with their feelings and let their minds go on vacation, and that's why the Christian religion has failed up to now." Man should "behave like Christ did but not like the preachers tell you to. . . . Carry your own church around inside of you and pray in it according to your needs." Carley does not say what man should pray *to*, only what he should pray *for*. He denies anything in religion smacking of obedience to something superior to the individual: men are not to "make their knees pliant before the Holy Ghost, or to emasculate their lives with a hopeful and joyous servility borrowed from the Bible." Carley's language hints that obedience to official religion and its God is symptomatic of sexual sickness, as well as intellectual, as the term "emasculates" suggests.

Independence from authority dominates the novel. Carley ridicules his parents and the judge who sentences him for insurance fraud. He rebels in jail, kicking his guards and mocking the warden who gives him "a paternal warning." John's father had, in fact, taught the morality leading to the son's thievery. He was a "belligerent, husky, flat-souled man who wanted his sons to go out and get what was coming to them," whose "hard face was gnarled and marked by the aftermaths of fights, apparently engaged in to get what he wanted." And John rebels from the authority of the books he has read, formulating his philosophy by rejecting them. And Selma too rejects authority: her parents are oppressive and vicious, and ultimately she leaves them and their ways. Her attitude toward religion is symbolized by the church bells she hears Sunday morning, after having slept with her boss, that "rang out . . . against each other in an effort to mesmerize the hearts of potential worshippers. . . . but no ear in the city block where she lived was able to detect the meanings behind them. . . . They were like the syllables of a big lie summoning the smaller lies of her day." She rejects her superiors at the Merry Grotto and at the millinery shop. This rejection of authority—social, religious, political, parental—recurs throughout Bodenheim's work.

In the most dramatic portion of the book, Carley confronts a brutal, hypocritical society by forcing it to recognize the absurdity of its nature. Attempting to enter the Merry Grotto in his worker's clothes—the regular patrons are made to wear coats and ties—Carley is beaten and thrown out. He returns to explain his theories to the bosses with extended hand, smiling and saying "Don't you want to be a friend of mine?" Ravanni, the boss, and his two chief assistants pounce on him again and punch his face and body. Again he lies thrown out, and again he returns smiling. As often as he is beaten, he returns, grinning through his puffed lips and offering his hand in friendship. The hoodlums feel he is "disputing the backbone of their lives and . . . must be adequately punished before their erectness could return."

Finally, Carley crawls up the steps after a particularly vicious beating and says "'Can't you see that it's impossible to kill my desires? When you're tired of hitting me we'll sit down and talk to each other . . . .' Once more they hurried him down the hallway, punched him wearily, and flung him down stairs. Once more he arose and ascended the stairs, with his friendly formula intact, climbing them painfully, one by one." The hoodlums now admit Carley to the Merry Grotto, partly from admiration for his physical courage and partly "to question the mystery" he presents them. Carley's apparently gratuitous and insane sacrifice accomplishes its purpose. The three toughs—the owner especially—have been puzzled and shocked into thought. They soon listen to Carley's arguments that their unreasoning hatred of him is far more absurd than his obsessive attempts to startle them out of hatred. When Ravanni's assistant Liscenco declares "Well, either he's crazy 'r we are," Carley appears temporarily effective.

The remainder of the novel concerns Carley's relationship with Selma. Her first attraction is physical, and her sexual impulses seem as neurotic as the old were habitual: "She wanted him with a fervor like that of a raptly chastised nun, who had disrobed herself before a vision of the Savior and felt that a gigantic command had destroyed the forbidden welcome of sin. Taking him wouldn't be like taking another man." Despite Carley's assurance of love, Selma is unable to withstand the tensions of no sex her secular Christ imposes and after a month disappears from the Merry Grotto and temporarily from Carley's life. Carley, who decides she must return to him freely, makes no attempt to find her. Instead, he returns to his philanthropic thievery, parodying society's avarice by stealing from it, just as he had parodied its brutality by forcing his own beating at the Merry Grotto.

When Selma ultimately becomes strong enough to leave her family, Carley better understands the physical needs of both himself and Selma. Unmarried, she and John begin a Robin Hood's tour of cities that ends in John's arrest. Placed in an insane asylum for what he calls "exalted paranoia—grandiose inflation of ego not shared by neurologists," John escapes and returns to Selma. He explains to her that he must continue his mission of forcing men to face themselves, and that he realizes that the next time he is apprehended stealing, he will be placed under more strict security—not for his crimes, but for his social subversion. He will be recognized by society "as an incurable case of intelligence." In prison he will think and write, and Selma will visit him with "the reports and retorts" of her life, she will give herself physically to men and women but listen to no words except his. Hearing this vision, Selma wonders about her future role. But "unannounced and mysterious, a quietness transpired within her." She says, "I don't even know why," and becomes his first disciple, "perhaps a little crazy" herself.

Despite the faulty ending—one can almost hear chimes ringing as Selma decides to stay with Carley—*Crazy Man* is a better book than *Blackguard*. Bodenheim's best writing in the novel is his portrayal of Selma, a girl who had cut herself off from fulfilling family and social contact, who has no religious or moral discipline to aid her rebellion, and who would ordinarily be doomed to a life of empty recalcitrance in contemporary urban civilization, so thoroughly has she been pressed by its mold. Carley is less successfully described, but Bodenheim had created a distinct and interesting Christ figure at a time when Christ was practically a cliché in fiction.

Bodenheim is still gabbily omniscient in the book, but his simple three-part structure produces orderly progression; and, as a result, his philosophic interpolations are short; and he focuses effectively on key scenes. He again reveals a good ear for the depressingly banal tedium of poverty-stricken minds and for the equally petty and habitual language of family squabbling. "Now you stop jokin' with me," Selma's mother shouts; "I've always been a modest woman and I'm not ashamed of it either but you sure didn't inherit none of it from me. Go on, now, put your nightgown on." Bodenheim's rococo descriptions are also frequently bright: "Lucille, in the atrocity of her pink dress with a melee of ruffles, and one hundred and seventy pounds of pale brown flesh that might have been used as a sail for some grotesque ship, for it presented a light and adventurous appearance in spite of its weight, and curved loosely outward."

The book's investigation of the viciousness of contemporary urban life is sharp, and its revelation of city behavior patterns, especially sexual, are significant and in greater part valid. The crippling effect of enforced closeness on the rootless yet circumscribed city dweller, the futile and frenzied habitual search for "kicks," the ugliness of city life and bleakness of city hopes, continue Bodenheim's portrait of the American wilderness.

VIII *Projects and Hopes*

But these early novels did not sell well, and poetry sales were negligible. As his publisher Horace Liveright wrote him concerning *Introducing Irony*: the book "hasn't sold, but good poetry rarely sells in the life-time of the poet. . . . I'm going to break my neck to sell the 1000 copies which we printed. . . . Together we should be able to get up the sort of advertisement that would shame the would-be intellectuals into buying your books." Early in 1922 Bodenheim had tried what Louis Grudin called one of the "least fantastic" projects for making money on his writing, a privately printed book of stories to be called, in Bodenheim's words, "*Seven Sneers*, A group of weird whispers and grins that revel, impartially, in the mud and beauty of life. . . . [to] include Mr. Bodenheim's signature, personally written in pen and ink, [and] his photograph. . . . *Seven Sneers* is original as a green-feathered visitor from Mars, as daring as an intellectual machine-gun." In his mock-brochure for the project, which unfortunately never materialized, Bodenheim refers to himself as "original, eccentric, sardonic, and with an intellect like an intangible razor. He stands alone in American literature, belonging to no school or clique and with a style that cannot be traced to any living writer."[16]

One place Bodenheim was moderately happy—for him—was the MacDowell Colony in Peterborough, New Hampshire. He worked there during the summers of 1921, 1922, 1923, and 1925. His first year at the colony, Bodenheim wrote his wife that Edwin Arlington Robinson—whose work and stoicism Bodenheim admired—had immediately suggested, upon seeing his application, admitting Bodenheim to the summer retreat. Over the years Bodenheim worked in relative peace at MacDowell, writing poems, plays, and novels; playing billiards and talking with Robinson, who once claimed that soon the bemused skeptic would be writing conventionally rhymed and metered verse. The taciturn Robinson and the flamboyant, garrulous Bodenheim saw the brutal world in much the same way; but Bodenheim appreciated Robinson's disciplined stance against the universe.

Bodenheim flirted as always—Stephen Vincent Benét cheerfully reported to Rosemary Benét that the art colonists were "diverted by the fact that young Richard Untermeyer removed the young lady that Maxwell Bodenheim had been devoting attention to, right from under Maxwell's nose." Yet Bodenheim sent long letters home to city-bound Minna lamenting how much he missed her and reporting what he was writing. Once he wrote her two hours after he had arrived, and always he begged for letters from her to match his. To Louis Grudin he wrote one letter amusing in its ripe rhetoric, until one realizes how absolutely dependent Bodenheim was on contact with his wife: "Dear Lou, I have not heard from Minna for two weeks now, and a worried telegram which I sent her two days ago has not been answered. In God's name what has happened? I am too agitated now to write a very coherent letter. Worry, a crude monster who knows the softer places of the heart, has honored me with his visit, and I have written almost nothing on my novel this week."

Though Bodenheim was not a model guest, Mrs. MacDowell thought him talented; and she felt she could cope with his idiosyncrasies for the sake of art. Bodenheim, who sometimes felt he was only tolerated, once wrote his wife bitterly, yet with comic understanding, about how one of the administering staff had told him they were happy to accommodate many kinds of people at the colony—the talented gentlefolk, and his kind too. When he thought himself too much in a smugly artistic Philistia (he was deeply humiliated, for example, by being unable to fly or take the train to New York occasionally, as some of the other guests could), he rebelled. Once he drunkenly broke into a town dance. Fighting an attempt to throw him out, he claimed immunity by right of being a colony member. And he always kept his room dirty and sloppy: Elinor Wylie once stoutly refused to sleep in the same bed that Maxwell Bodenheim had profaned. But still, life was generally quiet and healthy, and his artistry was respected, if not worshiped.[17] The 1923 *Peterborough Anthology*, a colony retrospect, edited by Jean Wright and Herbert S. Gorman, contained five of Bodenheim's poems: E. A. Robinson had the same number included.

Bodenheim's non-colony life of the period, however, showed little of the bucolic pastoral. He tried to support his poetry and family by fiction, and in 1923–24 by newspaper work on Ben Hecht's gusty *Chicago Literary Times*. But what was one of many money-making enterprises of Hecht, turned into another fiasco for Bodenheim.

CHAPTER 3

Man on a Seesaw

BODENHEIM traveled to Chicago happily enough. He was returning to the scene of his discovery, reuniting with Ben Hecht, and had a new publisher for his poetry and novels, Boni and Liveright. Bodenheim's grievances against Harcourt, Brace, who had published *Crazy Man*, included the standard complaints: they were "niggardly . . . ferocious penny squeezers" who "turned me down for an advance royalty at a critical moment and in spite of a fervent statement of need" and who were "chicken-hearted in support of my work." Liveright, on the other hand, wrote Bodenheim he had "devised a really brilliant scheme for immediately circularizing and putting over publicity stuff on the next novel [*Replenishing Jessica*], thus creating a gradually ascending momentum of interest that will sell out the first edition advance orders before the book is actually published."

Bodenheim, who worked hard for the *Chicago Literary Times*, cut his drinking so he could work even harder: "Had a little gin at a party in Ben's room, and it has had a bad effect on my energy today," he wrote Minna; "I see that I may even have to cut out occasional indulgences." His salary at first was about twenty dollars a week, and he managed to fill a few lecture dates to add to his income. He cut expenses to the bone, and sent what he could to New York for his wife and child. Much later, Mrs. Bodenheim joined him, and they both worked, while Solbert was placed in a country school in Wisconsin. As associate editor, Bodenheim wrote about half the paper and sometimes more; but he also enlisted New York friends, such as Louis Grudin, to send articles and letters.

The magazine prospered at first, and Bodenheim optimistically wrote Grudin that "our last issue . . . was an eight page one, and we are planning to eventually raise it to sixteen pages. We are getting in advertisements, and our number of two weeks ago sold 8,000 copies. . . . the present prospects look very good. If it goes I'll eventually have a salary of a hundred a week and all secondary honors." Bodenheim even found time to write, with Hecht, the travails of "Cutie, a Warm Mamma." The amusing novelette, privately printed, concerned a happily fallen woman so sexy that she "left a trail of asterisks when she walked," and the super smut-hound Rudolph Pupick, who at five months refused to nurse at his mother's breast because the act was immoral.

Through May, 1924, Bodenheim received no regular salary. Hecht's wife Marie claimed that Bodenheim's room and board at the Hecht's was equal to at least twenty-five dollars a week. (At the time, Bodenheim managed to send Minna twenty dollars a week— sometimes—by including his lecture money.) Bodenheim collided several times with Hecht, demanding more money for son Solbert's maintenance and for Minna, who before she came to Chicago had a physical breakdown in New York. When Hecht insisted that Bodenheim wait until the paper was more firmly established, Bodenheim refused to submit his wife and child to "glowing promises" any more, and threatened to quit. Hecht temporarily relented, and for a time he paid Bodenheim regularly.

The journalism Bodenheim wrote for the *Chicago Literary Times* was of high order. While he occasionally wrote rhapsodic prose-poems of little sense or value, he far more frequently wrote sprightly, witty, and sometimes spiteful articles about his own life (or his life as he imagined it) and about the artistic world around him. He described literary parties he attended, "Greenwich Village Spots," as well as friends he liked and disliked. In a *Village Voice* interview Hecht once admitted that he read only the lead of most Bodenheim articles before having them set in type; but later, when he reread the material, he recognized it as excellent journalism. If Bodenheim had been temperamentally suited to maintain the pace of disciplined journalism, he clearly would have had the talent to succeed.

Instead, his financial troubles increased and he and Hecht argued more. Bodenheim spent so much time on the paper that he could not write the poems and novels he lived for. In his romantically self-lacerating letters to Minna and friends he despaired. He wrote to Minna: "Life is a horde of self-immersed dwarfs, and one must grimly raise ones shield in an endless fight with them, or perish." Some hope re-emerged when Horace Liveright thought he might take over the paper, but a lawyer named Blonder bought it instead. Bodenheim still avoided the bars and somehow found time to complete *Jessica,* but at considerable expense to his wiry body. He realized that the old Chicago of his youth was gone, and that he could no longer play the terrible child. "Chicago's Bohemia is dead; cabarets are sickening affairs to me; and otherwise my few pounds of energy must be frantically hoarded," he wrote Minna. Meanwhile, "is dearest Solbert pink and happy? Give him some fiery kisses for me."

Then Chicago's terrible spring of 1924 came, bringing only more cold and promises; and Bodenheim knew that this summer he could not go to MacDowell Colony. He wrote Minna, "for the past three summers, I have been so used to quietness while creating that I am afraid the novel will falter unless I can give it some degree of solitude." He would try to rent a shack on the dunes, he told her, to write in solitude and warmth. And he worried about absent Minna's health, and about his teeth, decayed or blackened now, though he was only in his early thirties. He seemingly could never escape his past.

Then everything collapsed. On July 23 he wrote to Grudin from a furnished room on West Third Street, Manhattan, that he had "just returned to New York after a rather disappointing and dramatic period in Chicago. . . . As usual, I am very tired and desperately engaged in patching up rents in my armour. I am facing a drably sweating summer in this city, and the picture does not entice my religious sanction." In the letter's corner, an apparent afterthought, is "Minna is well and working in Chicago: the baby is at a country school in Wisconsin." On October 2, 1923, just before he had left for Chicago, he had written in momentary somberness to Grudin: "My life has been a dirty, cruel, involved, pummeled, crucified mess—with the exception of two, glittering hours." He also wrote, "well, I have made up my mind concerning one thing—if the clawing sincerity of melodrama, or sudden loss, ever descends upon me again, I shall desert the sleek jest of physical existence." Back in New York a year later, his perseverance belied the stilted wailing. But the slow striding to disaster continued, and it was foregone that his foot would slide in due time.

Somewhere in his early years, in that time of rebellion and shame, Bodenheim became an engine for destruction whose blades cut sharper within than without. Setting his goals impossibly high, he could find only failure. Needing some sort of stable family existence, he again and again left his wife and child. Almost paranoiacally obsessed with real or imagined rebuffs, he misused his friendships with Aiken, Burton Rascoe, and Grudin —needling the last two for their respectability, their middle-class social compromises, while borrowing from them. He behaved atrociously at gatherings; in fact, he did everything to destroy whatever relationships might have given him limited friendship or ordinary social identity. Having posed since his arrival on the literary scene as the tortured victim of a thousand conspiracies, he now forgot the difference between player and part. Although he cried like Job of his misfortunes and neglect, most saw him as his own tormentor, his own victimizer. Many who saw him as Max, the Bohemian Don Juan, did not realize that he lacked control over what he did to himself. Those few who recognized his essential helplessness, and that his outcrying against shams and hypocrisies of all kinds perhaps included himself, still remained his friends.

So, while Bodenheim was recognized as a significant figure during the 1920's, while a few of his books finally began to sell—*Replenishing Jessica* about forty thousand copies and *Georgie May* about thirty-five thousand—Bodenheim thought of himself as neglected by critics, acquaintances, and public alike. In his own eyes he was a failure as husband, father, and writer. To a sick friend he wrote in March, 1927, "I am a distinguished outcast in American letters—a renegade and recalcitrant, hated and feared by all cliques and snoring phantom celebrities, from ultra-radical to ultra-conservative—an isolated wanderer in the realm of intellect and lithely fantastic emotion, hemmed in by gnawing hostilities and blandly simulating venoms." Those like Grudin and Minna, who realized he was being sucked down in a whirlpool whose power he increased himself, could at least account for his behavior, if not always endure it. To many others, however, he became a literary bum, a cultural anarchist, or a satanic Bohemian.

Several events contributed to the Bodenheim image during the

1920's. Before this time, many anecdotes portrayed Bodenheim as the bumbling Raggedy Andy, such as the story concerning him and Amy Lowell.[1] The Lady Bountiful of Imagism invited ragged Bodenheim to her house for poetry and food. He arrived early and Lowell's dogs attacked him, ripping his already shreaded scarecrow's clothes (the same dogs had attacked Randolph Bourne, incidentally). Under his plate at dinner the rescued Bodenheim found a ten-dollar check. He demanded ninety dollars more to calm his nerves by a trip back to Chicago. Bodenheim had then been "a figure to look up to," one writer told Allen Churchill.[2] Suddenly the stories were not so innocent: "suddenly he was a man to be avoided."

Replenishing Jessica damaged his reputation, though it increased sales. In July, 1925, the professional smut-hunter John S. Sumner brought charges against Bodenheim and Horace Liveright for publishing the allegedly obscene and pornographic book. The charge was ridiculous, and the defense consisted mainly of reading the book to the jury. Newspapers described how the jurors slept through supposedly juicy passages, and Mayor Jimmy Walker astutely remarked that no girl had ever been seduced by reading a book. Liveright was acquitted and sales jumped. But Bodenheim was labeled thereafter as a writer of dirty books, a charge one still sees. Bodenheim himself was depressed by the trial. Originally delighted by his affront to the New York Society for the Supression of Vice, he was disappointed in what he considered Liveright's betrayal. Bodenheim was shunted to Chicago and Milwaukee during the testimony, though he strongly wanted to testify. He also wrote bitterly to his wife that, had he been someone like Theodore Dreiser, his publishers would have presented him as a hero. Instead, they exculpated themselves by claiming the manuscript he had brought them was far less clean than the one they eventually published.[3]

What the public heard of Bodenheim fortified his status as Don Juan. With the equally self-destructive millionaire Robert Clairmont, Eli Siegal, author of the poem "Hot Afternoons Have Been in Montana," and John Rose Gildea, Bodenheim was supposed to have become a member of the "Greta Garbo Social Club," which had the avowed intent of systematically seducing all unvirtuous innocents who bobbed like so many ripe apples in the liberated

Village barrel. Bodenheim's reputation gave him the aura of delightful wickedness that one variety of silly girl could find perversely thrilling. Clearly, however, the girl most likely to throw herself—one imagines giggling—into his bed, was exactly the kind he most disdained. Ben Hecht in *Gaily, Gaily* depicts him at parties leering obscenely at inaccessible matrons, and others report his playing the erotic fool when he was bound to meet only digusted rebuff, which is perhaps unconsciously what he sought. Occasionally, he would bed some foolish girl out for kicks. A publisher's agent confided to me that Bodenheim would send these on trivial errands for him so they would be seen and humiliated.

I Replenishing Jessica *(1925)*

The book that contributed most to Bodenheim's reputation as a libertine was *Replenishing Jessica*. Jessica's erotic rebellion is her chief weapon against an immoral society. But, unlike Selma Thallinger, she is essentially corrupted by her behavior; and Bodenheim portrays her decline with increasing distaste. Jessica, a sexual Lanny Budd, sleeps with over a dozen men from two continents and various social worlds, attempts to split her sex life from the rest of her existence, but becomes increasingly coarsened and degraded. Occasionally, a bright phrase shines through the repetitious and frequently dull narration of Jessica's sex life—for example, the book's most notorious image: "his fingers enveloped the fullness of her breasts quite as a boy grasps soap-bubbles and marvels at their intact resistance"—but generally the book is disappointing unless perhaps read as "hot stuff" in very early adolescence.[4]

The book's main failure is Bodenheim's strange social and psychological naïveté. For all its quasi-mystical meandering, *Crazy Man* was solidly rooted in a drab and oppressive milieu that exerted a strong force over its characters. Carley himself could be analyzed as a case of dementia praecox, or as a kind of holy bum. In *Replenishing Jessica* Bodenheim does not present a credible world to warp Jessica into her rebellion. The picture Bodenheim gives of the rich is thin and unconvincing, certainly too weak to account for Jessica's intense promiscuity. Jessica herself is worth four million dollars, and this fact simply does not function in the novel. The weight of so much money should seriously be accounted for in such a supposedly gorgeously crippled life. And Bodenheim's chronic disregard of Freudian psychology permits him to neatly separate from the causes of Jessica's dilemma the facts that she was the only child of a millionaire father and that her mother had been dead for several years. Though she is sexually attracted to her father and has censored out remembrance of her mother, Jessica's relationship to her parents "had little effect on [her] make-up," Bodenheim tells us.

Bodenheim succeeds better with some of his minor characters, second-rate artists and poets. Ted Purrel, Jessica's first husband, who combines a simple acquisitive mentality with brutal sexuality, is reminiscent of Scott Fitzgerald's Tom Buchanan. Purrel has wealth without wisdom and earns far more money than he needs. He eventually wallows in lust but demands strict propriety from his wife, whose luster as a property-object of others' envy he does not want tarnished. Bodenheim accurately pegs the poverty of Ted's mind: "you're the bee's mustache," he tells Jessica, "the beetle's bandana, the turtle's requiem." But the minor characters do not redeem what is too often a silly and sometimes frivolous book. Bodenheim depicts neither the forces of society nor of the mind with sufficient serious intensity to make Jessica meaningful. The social world appears irrelevant to her motivation, and her mind and body are insulated from what would be in real life the shock of her decline.

II Ninth Avenue *(1926)*

His next novel was less sensational and far better written. *Ninth Avenue* provides what Bodenheim had been heading toward in his first three fictions, an almost classic example of the American city novel.[5] Urban ugliness frames and dominates the book, which opens in the concrete-hard light of a city Sunday morning and closes with its heroine Blanche and her Negro lover gazing hopefully beyond the dirty green swells of the Hudson River. In between, the city forces its imprint on all characters and events. The novel's first paragraph describes the "smudged, flat fronts" of tenements that seem like "warehouses stretching down both sides of the street . . . holding commodities rather than human beings." Through this depersonalized squalor roams the Ninth Avenue elevated train, mechanical, saurian, overpowering, yet itself dwarfed by the cold towers surrounding it. And its tracks do not lead beyond the city, only through it. It goes nowhere.

Blanche Palmer's New York is not an inert backdrop symbolizing an enemy of the people but a real agent of misery and evil. Its Hell's Kitchen filth, the cheaply erotic shuffling and ragtime of its Dreamland dance hall, the numbing gin and jazz of its Golden Mill—all combine to exert tremendous pressures upon the hapless individual. These pressures are unrelievable except, some characters hope, through sex; but in the city sex is furtive, hasty, joyless. Life is mechanical and dehumanized. Taxis dart "like feverish insects." Trains crawl "soddenly packed with underdogs" beneath the "yawning, meanly barrack-like" city architecture. The train tracks themselves stretch "like a still millipede, with smaller insects shooting over its back." Communication between individuals is replaced by bleary indifference, and only ersatz romance exists.

Cruelty abounds in such a world, for the male can assert his individuality only through violence or by some other display of power, especially through sex domination. The women seek temporary escape through titillations and thrills, but they must be careful not to succumb too easily to the predatory male. Girls and boys are wise in the ways of grasping pleasure and are sexually knowledgeable too young. Blanche's sister Mabel is at eighteen "stuffed with tricks, and informations, and cool wiles picked up on streets and cabarets." Older standards of value have largely disappeared, and institutions such as church and family have little pressure to exert. Ritual is conventionalized and trivialized: somewhat like Alexander Pope's Belinda, Blanche "combed her dark red, bobbed hair, as though it were a sacred and perilous performance." She performs these rites on Sunday morning. Sunday has become in fact a travesty. Blanche's family is stolidly content together once a week, after Sunday dinner, when they are physically if not spiritually full.

While the city is large, for Blanche and her family it is as repetitious as their lives are narrowly circumscribed. Ninth Avenue itself winds insidiously throughout the book like the great Chinese Wall reminding Blanche that escape is difficult, if not impossible. Moreover, the avenue keeps the barbarians within, not without. Wherever she goes, the avenue on which she lives is not far away. She scuffs her way home from work on Ninth Avenue; strolls carelessly along the evening street to meet her date who also works as a clerk on Ninth Avenue; plods home down Ninth Avenue from the unsatisfying dream world of the movies; sluggishly boards for home the Ninth Avenue elevated after breaking with one boyfriend; and struts down the avenue with another unsuccessful suitor. As she becomes educated to her predicament, she walks with disgust along the street, hoping that "at last she had a chance to leap from the greasy, colorless weights of Ninth Avenue." But, until she is about to flee the city, she cannot escape the street and all it represents. Such retreats as Bryant Park provide only momentary relief. And endlessly over the city other avenues strand the web trapping the individual. Looking at Fifth Avenue from the steps of the New York Public Library, she watches the "endless stream of crawling, shiny, smoothly soulless automobiles."

Like Dreiser's Sister Carrie, Blanche is largely an inarticulate seeker, wondering about her status in an environment that nebulously dissatisfies her. "Something that was not wisdom but rather an engrossed search for wisdom" rests in her face. She wanders through New York aimlessly, yet questioning. "She didn't know where she was going, but she wanted to imagine that she was searching for some destination that would greet her unexpectedly." But she must grow up intellectually before she realizes what she is searching for. Until that time, she only knows there is "too much bossing in the world," that nothing "honest and good" exists in the life around her. Blanche's quest, initiation, and rebellion provide the focal points about which the book is organized.

Blanche's passionless sexual conquests reaffirm the emptiness of her life and the inhumanity of city life in general. One by one, men provide her with an idea or two, or momentary thrills; but their main function is to educate, not love her. Louis Rosenberg, a young man interested in *"higher literature,"* works in a library where he can borrow books and ideas. A "pleasant 'schlemiel,'" Rosenberg helps sharpen and make more articulate Blanche's rebellion. Partly under his tutelage the poverty of Blanche's speech —"Gee, but you're the cat's something. I wish you had more get-up about you"—decreases as her powers of observation increase.

Rosenberg also underscores one of the book's main themes. His discussion of a novel called *First Street* clearly shows that Ninth Avenue is another Main Street. The metropolitan city exceeds Gopher Prairie in violence and danger, but it is just as much a culturally blasted trap. Blanche also has affairs briefly with Joe Campbell and Fred Roper. The first, a flashy vaudevillian, is a grosser Drouet; and the second, a gambler. Both are pretenders to power and are soon to be cast-off products of the city's materialistic drives. None of the three can crack the protective shell that immures Blanche from self-fulfillment.

Blanche slowly learns to recognize and communicate her oppression. Early in the book she had only dimly perceived the crude flaws in her family, but she becomes increasingly critical. (Self-realization in Bodenheim's novels is almost always accompanied by a highly critical view of one's family.) She sees her mother as weak; her father, brainless; her brother, a bully; her sister, a deceptive gold-digger. Where formerly she dated men like Roper, carefully balancing the "lurking risk" of seduction against the feeling of importance their interest provides, she grows to realize that sexual attraction in itself is an unworthy and unsatisfying goal. Blanche displays throughout the book more sexual credibility than some of her literary sisters, such as Sister Carrie. Unlike such a dreamy, unknowing seeker, Blanche is sexually knowledgeable. She knows the rules of the game she plays and is prepared to take the risks. She does not drift sexually, she is never sexually stupid, innocent, naïve: the city teaches everything about sex except the human values it involves.

Blanche's final rebellion from the city is foreshadowed in her complete break from the family. Although she is always somewhat independent of them, she does not until late in the novel decide that she must separate herself absolutely from their swinish morality. Her integrity demands that she operate outside the confines of what slight bit remains of the family tradition of community. Her bickering, defeated, city family hearkens back to that of Crane's *Maggie* and forward to Farrell's O'Neills and Lonigans. All that remains of their hollow religion (Presbyterian) is a hard shell of bigotry: "Guess you're goin' out tonight with that Jew-kike of yours," brother Harry says. "Can't you pick out somethin' better than a Christ-killer, huh?"

Blanche's parents are vestigial, offering no real guidance, only viciously utilitarian platitudes. The mother whines helplessly "marry, marry," hoping that her girl will marry well before she becomes known as damaged goods. The father is a weak brute able to scream only the emptiest of threats. Harry is a petty thug and crooked prizefighter who fears that disclosure of Blanche's suspected (and to him profitless) immorality will reflect badly upon him. Her other brother, Phillip, has "the face of a sneaking philanderer." His personal philosophy is that "you can't be a goody-goody and come out on top in this burg. . . . I don't believe in stealing 'r holding anybody up, but just the same you've got to be as tricky as the other side, I'm telling you." Unfortunately, like his father and brother, Phillip is not tricky. He is trained to accept the urban idea of success, but he is too stupid to achieve it. Blanche's sister Mabel is the family's moral ideal. She dates only rich men who can take her to expensive places. She carefully, or so she thinks, metes out physical rewards for services rendered; appears discreet; and at eighteen seems to know just how far to go to catch the wealthy sucker. She is herself, however, hooked without even knowing it.

The family generally is too stupid and insensitive to be successful in anything and too corrupt to practice common humanity. Bound by conventions meaningless to it, the family's only redeeming quality is its clannish defense, occasionally, of some family member. The members are cave dwellers whose only sense of belonging is to their cave. They bluff and threaten, and whine and snipe at each other with heavy sarcasm, all of which Bodenheim describes depressingly well and in detail. Their ethics are muddled about the proposition how much each can get and how little each can give for it. Pressed together by a hostile environment, they imitate hostility, though they are often powerless to enforce their antagonisms. Described as "upper-proletarian," they have Ninth Avenue "stamped into their spirits." Blanche's responsibility to herself demands that she vanish from their circle.

The novel loses force temporarily when Blanche first breaks with her parents. The work's last third shows Blanche's adventures in Greenwich Village Bohemia and her romance with the Negro poet Eric Starling. Bodenheim's journey into the Negro problem and miscegenation is interesting, but life in the Village never seemed duller. Blanche first meets in the Village Max Oppendorf and Ben Helgin. These characters serve thematically to further her education by making her realize the wideness and variety of the world outside Ninth Avenue, New York. Oppendorf helps her articulate her nascent powers of observation, and, partly under his tutelage, she sells a few prose sketches to magazines.

But all too obviously Oppendorf and Helgin are transparencies for Max Bodenheim and Ben Hecht. As Oppendorf, Bodenheim compliments himself: "a recognized poet and novelist, he was nevertheless known as a distinguished outcast, ostracized . . . because of his skillful-tongued independence." He also tries to destroy several Bodenheim myths by attaching them to Oppendorf and ridiculing them. He denies in this way that he is a rapist, that he is a fake draft dodger (this for the benefit of radical friends who wanted him to be a real draft dodger), and that he periodically falls drunkenly down stairs. Helgin-Hecht is described as an esthetic Babbitt, a "watchman, ever alert in front of a towering but shaky house of cards." Satisfying as this sniping may have been to Bodenheim, it had no place in a serious work of fiction.

Fortunately Bodenheim soon dropped the Hecht squabble and began using experiences from Village existence that could be related thematically to *Ninth Avenue*. Blanche attends with Helgin a racially mixed party, almost consciously as a ritual commemorating her new life. At the party she dances with a Negro, something she would not have done before her change. By the time of the party she is beginning to substitute a fresh and reasoned morality for her thoughtless, habitual one. This rational morality permits her to see Starling, a poet and publicist, as a man first and a Negro second. Accepting the new attitude is not easy, but she finally realizes that she must leave her old world completely and attempt to find some sort of satisfaction with Starling, not in his world as Negro, but in a new life they will have with trouble to create themselves.

Bodenheim's investigation of the Negro is never simplified, as his sharpness describing motives at the mixed party indicates. Most of the people there, Negro and white, attend through a kind of reverse bigotry or obligatory but actually unfelt liberalism. His dramatization of Blanche's affair with Starling avoids many contemporary clichés of Negro fiction. Starling, for example, sometimes passes for white, and is no great crusader. He does not at first tell Blanche he is a Negro, he thinks from simple forgetfulness. But clearly he does not want her to know. Then he continues to pass for white with her, partly from fear of losing her, and perhaps to punish himself through his eventual discovery, and to punish her for being white. Blanche is stunned when he tells her, and she tries to sort out her conflicting emotions. She has, in fact, already revealed to Starling traces of her family's bigotry. After much debate with herself she decides she still loves him and wants to remain with him. But interestingly enough she does so because "he just didn't have the physical essence which she had always felt in the presence of other Negroes." Her choice is emotional and not reasoned. She still *feels* that he is white: "Yes, I know that he's a Negro," she tells a friend, "but you must admit, dear, that he's the whitest-looking one you ever saw."

Starling is genteel, basically unheroic, and a decidedly unprimitive Negro. He seems a realistic study of a non-militant Negro intellectual, and through him Bodenheim criticizes some liberal clichés. Starling attacks, for example, the unrealistic concept of the Negro in Carl Van Vechten's novel *Nigger Heaven*: "Even Vanderin isn't free from it. Take that latest book of his—*Black Paradise*. . . . He's just a bystander trying to be indulgent and sympathetic. It's the old story. Negroes are primitive and sa-avage at the bottom, and white people aren't . . . white people like your brother, I suppose," he says to Blanche. O'Neill's *All God's Chillun Got Wings* is also attacked for its insistence on inevitable, mystic, racial antagonism. Starling's un-negritude is itself shown when he suggests that only the intellectually exceptional Negro and white are equals. The others, Negro and white, apparently do not count. And the solution to Blanche's and Eric's specific dilemma is far from triumphant, though it has an air of reality. As the two look out over the Hudson, which had been "dirty" at the novel's start but which is a now slightly less terrible greenish gray, they grip hands "with the power of iron bands" as they begin life together. But they begin by escaping, by deserting their battleground: the novel hints that Eric is going to pass for white in Chicago's urban nightmare.

III   Returning to Emotion *(1927)*

Bodenheim returned to poetry for his next book, *Returning to Emotion*. In this work most of the limpness and flabby precocity that haunt his lesser poetry is gone. His lines are relatively firmer, tougher, more disciplined. The second poem in a series called "Chinese Gifts" suggests the poetically mature artist writing simply, unsentimentally, imaginatively. "Only fools believe/ That breezes shift the roses/ Within the valley of Hang Tso./ With lengthy whispers of perfume/ The roses command each breeze/ To tilt them in six directions." The poet sees a self-contained beauty in the roses so inspiriting that they appear to control the subservient wind. Only the ideally and not literally realistic poet can master this beauty: "Most poets in the valley/ Swear that the roses are tender,/ Frail, and smoothly amorous." The younger Bodenheim might have said this. However, "most poets" are wrong. "But one poet, derided by the rest,/ Insists that they are cold,/ Indiscreetly strong, and careless./ The roses alone bow to him."

The third poem in the series also chides Bodenheimian preciosity. When a cloud floats over the hills, two men strain at description. The first spins a tenuous image: "Invisible maidens, in dresses/ Blue and perfectly matched by the sky,/ Sometimes reveal their faces,/ Remembering a little, riotous dream/ Once confined in the valley." The second says in words reminiscent of Stephen Crane's cynical "A Man Said to the Universe": "This sprightly accident/ Is not recognized/ By the sky's tranquillity." A third man, who does not try to image the moment's effect, states briefly that such natural beauty is beyond verbal attempts to recapture. With "the fluttering prank of a smile on his face" he says: "Beauty is the instant/ When blended light and form/ Escape from domineering arguments."

"She Walks Down City Streets" similarly focuses on escape from domineering arguments and states a desire to return to the natural. This means for Bodenheim a return to natural emotions, to natural freedom of mind and thought that with simplicity disregards arbitrary social convention. He begins the poem with a direct statement of belief and then develops intensity of feeling not through fanciful imagery but through strongly phrased, explicit wording: "I have grown weary of the humorless,/ Unfairly strident and decrepit/ Conflict staged between disciples/ Of emotion and the mind,/ And all the squinting quibbles/ And ranting standstills of another fight/ Between the definitions/ Of poetry and prose." Bodenheim calls for free men, Whitmanesque wanderers, "the men who walk upon the hills,/ With faces cool, still, and aloof,/ With eyes whose sweeping straightness/ Emulates the stride of time,/ Beyond the rattling of bones."

Such a natural man is portrayed in "Daniel Boone," an unusual poem for Bodenheim that contains a nostalgic picture of his childhood, a period he almost never drew on for his poetry. He describes Boone simply, as a child might: "You were dressed in leather pants,/ With moccasins upon your feet,/ And on your head a round/ Coon-skin cap stood, and the tails/ Of the cap dropped to your back." The elemental frontiersman then stalks through a child's world of Indians: "Behind you an Indian lurked,/ Peering out from a bush,/ With feathers sticking straight from his hair,/ And naked save for a loin-cloth and war-paint./ He held his tomahawk/ Poised, and aimed it at your head."

Having dramatized a child's suspense, which he emphasizes in the enjambment of "He held his tomahawk/ Poised," Bodenheim suddenly withdraws the reader from the child's viewpoint by introducing the first fanciful metaphor of the poem, but one still involving a child's picture: "And my heart began to jerk,/ Like a fast but crippled acrobat." Then the reader discovers that the Boone scene is recollected from childhood, when the narrator was twelve and when the hero was "pictured crudely on the page/ Of a hectic, clumsy booklet." But even then the instinctive, natural Boone was recognized as a kindred spirit, "a poet/ Forced to use his eyes and muscles/ In the place of words and spoken rhythms."

Boone is a poet relying on his own natural impulses, an individualist seeking no aid from others. Another charming poem "Fairy-Tale," offers similar advice—be natural, self-reliant—to the artist. Bodenheim employs in it fanciful images, but this treatment is comic and so escapes didactic flightiness. "Fairy-Tale" tells the story of "The scullion of the queen" who is grieved that the queen "refused to lend a favorite sigh/ Of hers to stain the lightness of his cake." The scullion is the artist or poet who seeks inspiration

or aid outside himself, without relying primarily on his own resources. Playing with his images and placing them in effortless
and unobtrusive blank verse, Bodenheim employs an occasional
rhyme or trochee for emphasis, as when he continues the scullion's claims: "Boldly, he had demanded also one/ Long petal from
the winter of her mind,/ To serve as fertile icing for his tarts/
And one reproachful color from her heart/ To rescue the defi-
ciencies of taste." "Boldly" is a bold trochee, and "tarts . . . heart"
contrasts the artifact with the exterior influence. The queen, however, refers the poet-scullion back to "the tortured industry/ Of
his own imagination." Use that, she says; and he will "not need
the more/ Intangible corrections of a queen."

Another poem, "Caroline Speaks to Her Lover," satirizes un-
imaginative emotional orthodoxy and incidentally mocks sexual
intercourse as the only valid, ultimate communication between
lovers. Caroline mocks her conventional man: Shall we, she asks,
hear the wind, "only as a nervous ascension of lust,/ And see in
moonlight the swooning slavery/ Of emotions consumed/ By the
brightness of pain?" This response is the conventional, habitual
one of those "Whose buttocks slumber on the hill-sides," engaging
in "the frenzied rituals of men—/ The honored elephants of sexual
passion!" Rather, she says, "Let us meet as lightly as the air/
Which signals to this leaf above our heads." One should take
time, Bodenheim implies, and do what is emotionally right for
one. One should not just respond, a ludicrous passional elephant,
with the reflex conditioned by modern society.

"Here Is Your Realism" exhibits the darkness in man's emotions.
Like many of the poems in *Returning to Emotion* it is formally
constructed, employing iambic pentameter *abba* lines throughout,
as though underscoring that poems about emotion need technical
control, that rhapsodic or purposeless structure is inadequate to
focus content. This poem is also formally organized by being
treated as the criminal case it presents. Evidence of a murder is
examined in three sections, each an "Exhibit." "Exhibit A" is a
long knife; "Exhibit B," the rotting green-and-pearl face of a
murdered girl, her eyes bulging and lips drawn apart; "Exhibit
C"; "the man who strangled her/ Because her mangled, wrangling
heart became/ A greedy spectre, threatening him with shame."

In this American melodrama, the girl tells her lover to marry her or she will inform her father "what you did." So the man kills her, and now sits in his room "And spies a form upon the empty bed." Before he is discovered, he clinically examines his motives and reactions. The narrator of the case never himself reveals sympathy for the dead girl or condemns her killer. He simply examines the man's justifications, the girl's "Denouncing platitudes, Jehovah's wrath,/ And frenzied self-defences huddled close." Then the poet concludes with the killer's last feeling, egoistic and human: "She was nagging me./ If only she had kept her damn tongue still." This chases his sorrow for the deed: "And for an instant new resentments kill/ The swollen wraiths of guilt and perfidy." The poem again indicates Bodenheim's ability to use the violent contemporary scene in realistic poetry, to succeed in revealing a tabloid world that millions of normal, bloodthirsty Americans followed in famous murder trials of the 1920's, such as the notorious Hall-Mills case. Sometimes a platonist, Bodenheim needed to restrain a fine but occasionally nebular imagination. Through his city and crime poems, he helped invigorate the fragile and esoteric verse of his time.

But not all poems in *Returning to Emotion* do so. Some are fragile and esoteric themselves. "Lynched Negro" misses bitter social indictment and lapses into peripheral commentary: the Negro hangs unnoticed while the poet gestures to himself. "Songs to a Woman" never redeems—though it improves as it develops— the Pre-Raphaelite flimsiness of its opening New York City teahouse lyricism: "You are like startled song-wings against my heart/ Which flutter like a harp-string wounded/ By too much quivering music./ You cover me with a blue dream-robe/ Whose silk ripples out like imaged water." Such songs might please a young girl in love, but not a less emotional reader.

But few books of poetry that attempt anything worthwhile are perfect, and any such book should be judged by its successes. *Returning to Emotion* is often esthetically triumphant and demonstrates a poetically mature variety. Even in ordinarily less valuable areas, as with "Sonnet to Elinor Wylie," Bodenheim displays a hard, tight accomplishment. Among his early volumes, *Returning to Emotion* ranks high.

IV The King of Spain *(1928)*

The King of Spain reveals a general decline, however, from the arresting versatility of *Returning to Emotion*. Bodenheim reworks many old subjects with more gesture than force, and he is trapped at least once, in "Baseball Game," into revealing a style made pretentious by faulty application. In "Baseball Game" the pitcher views the batter "With a morbid cogitation/ Dressed in unconcern." At ball two, "The batter's scowl/ Remains but lessens to admit/ The lighter poise of confidence,/ And the pitcher surveys him/ With chagrin and anger—/ Twin playthings for his patient soul." The title poem, an overly long story of almost a hundred and fifty lines, concerns attempted regal assassination with ponderously allegoric overtones not really worth deciphering. Occasionally an attractive image flashes out, but it is too surrounded by bombast. One wonders if the plot were to talk the king to death, and then fondly hopes for its quick success. "Two Salvation Army Women" patronizingly points out that the wrong people have sponsored Christianity and describes one of these, a fat, middle-aged worker whose "lips are sensual moans/ Visible beneath the pretext/ Of your singing love for Christ."

"John Miljus Dies" tells of a worker crushed by a girder, but it generates neither sympathy for him nor recognition of class consciousness. The worker's death seems basically another opportunity for a poem, a chance for the poet to tap a few by now standard reactions. It does not successfully commemorate a valued life brutally destroyed. The failure is especially disappointing because the poem's start is promising, contrasting the coming of life, gaiety, and abandon with the constantly bleak world of worker John Miljus who is digging a hole: "Spring came on this morning/ With black-bottom, Charleston, and tango steps:/ Came not in venturings of pale green. . . ./ But leapt down the city block/ With gaieties rehearsed, sophisticated. . . ./ John Miljus slaved in the hole." But the poem too often lapses into direct prosy statement: "Oh, John Miljus, you are caught/ Between cynical and over-hopeful men/ Who gesture and argue while you chase/ Will-o'-the-wisps of freedom, peace." Too many images blur away from the final cutting vigor they need: "John Miljus in his rubber boots/ And overalls so like the color/ And texture of lost expectation."

Yet several shorter poems lift the volume from relative mediocrity. "Abstract Painting" offers in fairly terse alternate-rhyming lines of first iambic trimeter and then tetrameter an impression of what seems to be Cubistic painting. Bodenheim limns a puzzling portrait of one type modern woman, the destructive demi-*vierge*: "Life dyed her hair pale green,/ The color of a virgin's hate:/ Set purple on her lips—/ Decay and ripeness merged by fate. . . ./ She stained her face dark grey,/ The tinge beneath a harlot's grin." The taut lines limit Bodenheim's tendency to wander for effects, and only occasionally does he pad to meet metrical demands: "Her orange eyebrows held/ The arched inviting *known as* sin." (Italics mine.) Her grotesque coloring reveals to the keen eye the woman's essential nature. Critics see only the "insanely trivial," however, and the common clodman wants only to know "what's the joke."

"Circus" employs alternate line rhyme and blank verse in satirizing the fake emotional response that masks true reaction. Bodenheim describes first the grotesque and ludicrous circus where "An elephant profaned a dance: a girl/ Grinned in her lurid smugness on the backs/ Of horses, while a tall and whiskered churl/ Cracked whips to aid her." Then he describes audience response: a "vicious, jowled" man cries "Now I'm a happy boy again."

"The Steam-Shovel" continues Bodenheim's indictment of dehumanized contemporary life. The poem's narrator watches a steam-shovel that is in some ways more human than the man who operates it. The shovel "was an unsightly arm" with "a cupped hand with three crusted fingers./ The hand sank into earth and bulged with it:/ Then swung aloft in sudden exaltation." The man running the machine is less than human, with a "strained wet face and his eyes pressed to specks. . . ./ His face dead and dented like old tin." The narrator soon forgets the machine, but remembers the man, and remembers also another obsessed onlooker who watches the operation for over two hours, who says he "Can't seem to get enough of it."

"Advice to a Young Lady" employs tight organization and dramatic incident that lead to strange and effective metaphoric advice. Boccaccio, Don Juan, and Rabelais—the ribald, the artful lodger, the wild and free—all visit a young lady, whom the poet-narrator advises to offer compensation to each. To Boccaccio, she is to proffer a kind of purity; to Don Juan, forgetfulness of self; and to Rabelais, perhaps a free grace. Finally, Jesus Christ comes to the girl "In the midst of your lithe caracoles." Christ brings his own powers, "Pity and sternness squeezed into the straight gleam of his eye." Even to Christ the young girl can offer a gift: "Tell him to leap beside you/ Like a vainglorious Boy,/ Oh, tell him that austerity/ Needs only a dream of supple gaiety." The image repeats what the Christ figure of *Crazy Man* claimed, that Christianity neglects the free body.

In such a poem as "Advice to a Young Lady," Bodenheim imagines an odd, unreal situation; but, through restraint and fairly specific images, he dramatizes the emotional truth set forth: an individual needs emotional and intellectual completeness. And the young lady can give of herself physically or emotionally, but only when she has established some meaningful identity. The advice could apply as well to Bodenheim as artist. His poems reveal a compulsion to give of self, intellectually or emotionally. But occasionally only gestures, well known and gratuitous, are communicated. Too many of the poems in *The King of Spain* are gestures. Clearly, Bodenheim was at a stage of development where he needed to try something new.

CHAPTER 4

Before the Great Fall

BODENHEIM needed something new not only in his poetry but in his life, for the old life had become messy. In 1928 one of his girlfriends, Gladys Loeb, tried to kill herself after Bodenheim had rejected her. The eighteen-year-old stuck her head in a gas oven and turned on the gas, but her landlady found her, a copy of the poet's portrait clutched in her not-quite-dead hand. Perhaps as a direct result of this publicity, twenty-two-year-old Virginia Drew offered herself to Bodenheim. Late in their brief affair she threatened suicide but he dissuaded her. Inevitably she succeeded in drowning herself. Apparently disappointed that someone had triumphed where she failed, Gladys Loeb returned, followed by her father the doctor. A "Keystone Cops" comedy of chase, pursuit, and reconciliation was avidly reported by the papers as the affair shuddered into a very bad farce of the absurd.

Bodenheim's New York career gathered to it gratuitous and grotesque fragments of futile destruction as others acted out an expressionistic parody of his own life. Dorothy Dear (even the real name is improbable), with whom Bodenheim had corresponded, was killed in a subway crash. She was traveling to another meeting with Bodenheim, whose foolish love letters now littered the tracks. (To a woman absolutely an acquaintance and no more, Bodenheim once wrote: "I never came to know you as well as I wanted to, and that was because the squirmings and insinuations of surface sex too often intruded between us.") Aimee Cortez, who, enraptured, spun naked with a stuffed gorilla before bedding with the last man she pointed at, gassed herself, as had Gladys Loeb. She too clutched Bodenheim's picture, but no landlady discovered her in time. And Aimee Cortez had no particular involvement with Bodenheim, whom she had known mildly for several years.

Bodenheim escaped to Europe, where he wrote to Aaron Sussman: "I'm a hideously poor man, and if the novel [*Georgie May*] doesn't go over I don't know how I'll be able to meet the material scarecrows in my life."[1] Later he wrote Sussman: "If I cannot secure material ease and a decent sale with my novels, I might as well throw in the sponge. I have stopped work on my sixth novel [*Sixty Seconds*] and I am in a hopeless mood." Returning to Depression America in 1929, he gave crash-ruined Robert Clairmont a night of commemorative drinking. By 1931, *Naked on Roller Skates* had sold ten thousand copies and *A Virtuous Girl* another twelve thousand (both printed in 1930). Though some of Bodenheim's profits simply repaid advances, the books had sold well.

I Georgie May (*1928*)

Among the books of this period, *Georgie May* was Bodenheim's most successful fusion of action, style, and message. Georgie is a pre-World War I Memphis whore who wanders from one tough lover to another. Like many of Bodenheim's central women characters, she is sensitive and dreamy, but uneducated: an emotionally complex, quicksilver woman vulnerable to fits of deep despondency, since she exposes herself to greater emotional risks than the dumb, complaisant "chippies" about her. After the mother of her last, wealthy, upper-class lover throws in her face the folly of continuing such an impossible affair, Georgie decides "living was jus' a stinkin', bahstahd mess, and what in hell did a few yeahs moah oah less amount to anyway," and swallows poison. Every element in the book converges relentlessly toward this depressing climax. The conclusion is real and inevitable, not sentimentally melodramatic. Clearly seeing her fate and clearly recognizing the impassive cruelty of her world, she achieves a self-revelation that demands as a conscious act of will, her destruction. Her death becomes an act of self-assertion.

Bodenheim is occupied in *Georgie May* solely with delineating Georgie's destruction and with showing the brutality of the world that produced her; no peripheral plot exists, and there is no shifting of interest or focus as in his first books. The world that spawned Georgie is an accurately described Memphis hotpocket called "Rounder's Corner," a hangout for whores, thieves, addicts, and bums. Heat pounds through the novel—the dirty, heavy heat of a Southern city in summer. The book's second sentence focuses on the "dusty, heat flayed" stone and brick of Rounder's Corner, and thereafter most of the action festers under the pall of summer heat: "The heat began to make Georgie May comatose. . . . It pressed against her breasts till they took on a leaden sexlessness. . . . It made her legs seem ponderously useless." The "thick, brazen" heat is a major element of the novel's symbolic cosmos.

The Mississippi River further circumscribes movement. Its "turbid, brownish green" swells flow in imperceptible rhythm "grazing the presence of death." Like a "big brown snake," it coils ready to smash the levee or destroy the cane crop. Steamboats traveling on the river churn its water with "wounds of foam." Houseboats drift "along like uprooted homes." Other boats are like "parasites crawling up and down a narrow monster." No free Huck Finn, Georgie is able only once to leave the river-bound city, when she departs briefly with the foreman of a cotton mill. The rural settlement she inhabits is deadening in its unpastoral bleakness, and the city lures her back. Her habitual existence is too closely attuned to its vices and perversities. She is unable to escape a way of life she has been trained to need. Also walled on the river side by a hundred-foot bluff, the city is a prison no one in *Georgie May* ever really leaves. It is a state of existence, not merely a specific locale.

Like much of Bodenheim's best fiction, *Georgie May* is a city novel. It is one of the relatively few Southern city novels in a tradition dominated, as Gelfant's *The American City Novel* shows, by fiction about New York and Chicago. Bodenheim's ugly, cluttered Memphis weighs like a huge, heavy machine upon those crowded and trapped within; and it stamps out almost identically sordid lives. Drink, violence, and occasional flashes of lust temporarily relieve the oppressive tedium of the city's cage-weary animals. Georgie May slumps into an hotel armchair and flips through a paper she has read three times already. She paces in her seedy room over the worn, gray-threaded carpet, looks at the high-rodded brass hotel bed, at the blue china spittoons, and waits for that month's lover, a murderous dope peddler. With the "junkie" she finds violent, momentary, joyless release.

Outside in the city, hustlers and sex-ridden adolescent punks wander the slums. They prowl streets dwarfed by blocks of 'three and four-storey coops" past the detritus of decaying society: "wooden Indians holding out bunches of wooden cigars," past second-hand furniture stores, past a sign saying "artificial hair— rats, curls, wigs." In August's heat the dead "old whitely sprawl- ing, quaintly ample, dawdling South" suppurates. And Georgie May and her friends and lovers and bitter enemies squirm like maggots in the carcass of the city, the only home they are trained to endure. Bodenheim emphasizes this essential horror of city life: while it often destroys, it habituates its victims to destruc- tion. Rubbed raw by the city's harshness, Georgie cannot exist long in the peaceful mill town to which she tried to escape; and other characters who escape Memphis are invariably reported later in another similar city.

Georgie May is a typically lone and vulnerable character in her city environment. "Her only real, true-blue girl chum" is another prostitute, Emmy Lou; and this fanatically clinging friendship clearly cannot be anything but brief: Rounder's Corner is a male world. Separate from Emmy, Georgie weaves in and out of thieves' dens, "blind pigs," sleeps with one man or another, gets involved in a shooting, runs from the police, lives on the slope of the abyss. Twenty-three years old, she looks in a mirror and thinks "two or three years more and some men would be turning her down: five or six years more and she'd be scraping up the leav- ings." And she is no prostitute with a heart of gold; she is lazy, scheming, with a murderous temper. Yet, like so many of Boden- heim's women, she is both innocent and corrupt. "Must be two Gawgies," she say to herself. "One's lak ah was when ah stahted out, and t'othahs a fighting, boozing son of a bitch."

Georgie cannot resolve the split between her two selves. She cannot live satisfactorily as the young girl she was when she started out, or as the Rounder's Corner whore. She rejects mar- riage and babies and is only bruised by the decadent and sterile world of Rounder's Corner. This ironic split is reflected in a num- ber of related ironies the book contains, often juxtaposing some pleasant and unattainable situation with brutal reality. The very opening of the novel is ironic, for in the moist sizzle of August a middle-aged whore sprawls drunk on a bench waiting to pick

up some hobo, singing "In the Good Old Summertime." Bodenheim weaves throughout the book the comfortable banalities of
Tin Pan Alley, contrasting their sentimental unreality with Memphis life.

Prowling the streets after being turned out of her room because
her boyfriend wouldn't repay her the twenty dollars rent, Georgie
May sings in her mind "Billy McCoy was a musical boy, on the
steamer Alabama, steaming down to Yokahama." Huddling on a
Rounder's Corner bench she waits for a mark, humming "Why
don' yuh move lak me? Drink good whisky, babe, 'n get youah
pleasure free-e-e." Later she thinks of one night's score who
blubbered about his wife and mother and wonders how it would
be to stay with one man. She derisively hums "Call me up some
rainy aftahno-on. Ah'll arrange fo' a quiet littul spo-on. Think of
all the joy and bli-iss. We can hug and kiss and—talk about the
weathah."

Georgie May contains within herself other ironies. While waiting for a pickup, she smokes surreptitiously, glancing furtively up
and down the street. Policemen who may not mind her plying her
trade will not let her break the town's ordinance against women
smoking in public, and even Georgie feels half-guilty. Greater
irony is displayed in society's treatment of the criminal. Georgie
is jailed as a member of a dope ring, though actually she is only
tagging along with her latest lover, Dopey Watkins. Like her
fellow inmates, she is only strengthened in her anti-social attitudes and further educated in crime during her term. The jail is
the ultimate cage in a life of cages—the city, Rounder's Corner, an
apartment room. But none is as terrible as her cell, which is
simply a place that intensifies the life she leads "outside." She
determines that she will kill rather than return; and, when she
later discovers that life for her is in fact living in a cage, she kills
herself.

The jail sequence is important, for Bodenheim saw here a real
social evil, an inhumane manifestation of society more terrifying
than crime itself. He describes in detail a half-zoo, half-bedlam,
reporting its frightening sights and sounds. He records the "strangled" grunts of unmirthful laughter; the "smacks of slaps on bare
buttocks and bosoms." He describes the women's narrow rectan-
gular cages, constructed of iron and steel that sears the inmates'

skin during hot summer months. He notes the thin, straw-filled canvas pallets, the lice-encrusted walls, the moldy bread, and the chicory coffee.

Bodenheim carefully demonstrates the parallels between life in jail and in the city. In either prison, people are dehumanized, reduced to animals with yet enough reason to be tortured by thinking of their condition. Sitting in a "blind pig," Georgie sees her communication with others as "canines biting a little at each other's haunches, but staying the full power of teeth." A minor character has "the sensation of a dog, stopping after a skirmish with another snarling, unbending dog." The women in jail are more dangerous animals: like lions and wolves, they roar and bark. Bodenheim also offers many specific details of city life and jail life. He packs the book with incidental minutiae about jail menus and how food is slopped out and what coke-sniffing symptoms are, and thereby he richly corroborates his outrage.

Bodenheim's omniscience is less obtrusive than usual; it becomes an integral part of the book. From his first authorial outburst: "Oh Georgie May, did they give you rubbish and call it sweet, these kettle-bellied, rancidly kind owners of earth"; to the last inevitable "Oh Georgie May, the lurid, pent-up, vilified joke has ended"; the reader can easily recognize the choric if occasionally sentimental purpose of the author's words. Bodenheim's interpolations lament without interrupting. He integrates the personal passages with each other by phrasing them in a distinct style, usually beginning with the ritual phrase "Oh Georgie May." The sections become a conventionalized pattern within the fabric of the book itself, highlighting but not intercepting the pattern of the plot. The comments are as much a part of the novel as are the "Camera Eye" sections of John Dos Passos' *U.S.A.*

Generally, then, *Georgie May* is Bodenheim's tightest novel. His control of technique and attitude enables him to project powerfully the inevitable death of a young prostitute. He portrays only her life and nothing peripheral to it, and he attacks only those social problems that are relevant. The gratuitous anger so common in Bodenheim's work is absent. In his picture of underdog life in a Southern city he depicts enough details of everyday existence to enable the reader to draw close to objects of his convincing sympathy. His use of certain basic symbols of entrapment—the cages, the encircling river ready to strike, the high bluffs—and his counterpoint of ironic songs and parallels are similarly effective.

Several elements weaken the novel. Bodenheim writes most of the book's dialogue in pseudo-phonetic speech. For example, when Georgie's friend Emmy Lou reminisces about her childhood she remembers snatches of song: "Ah met him 'side the gahden gate 'n we swoah we'd nevah paht. . . . Ah'm a lil' rose, growing weah the sof' win' blows." This rendering is accurate enough for a novel, though "growing" would not have a final "g." But, even when the book was written, literary and public interest in such dialect reportage was generally slight. Occasionally Bodenheim employs stereotypes. Indicating the disparity between Negro and white, he employs a literary chestnut. "The white singers were strident and usually a little out of tune; the Negroes sang harmoniously, with a heart-squeezing, heavily liquid lilt," as their songs "invade" Rounder's Corner. This description comes perilously close to a similar one of white and Negro singing in O'Neill's *All God's Chillun Got Wings* (1924), a play whose racial falsity Bodenheim criticized in *Ninth Avenue*. Yet when he reports Georgie May's attitude toward Negroes, Bodenheim writes realistically of a lower-class white feeling. "Don' love 'em," she says, "don' hate 'em. . . . caint stand their skin but feel for them when they're suffering. People down and out got to feel for each other, just got to. Well-dressed, uppity niggah servants, now that was different."

Possibly the most serious objection concerning the philosophy implicit in the novel is that Bodenheim produces, as he often did, a false dilemma through his nihilism. Life on Rounder's Corner is wretched, he seems to say; but so is every other kind of attainable life. Being a prostitute is bad because it leads to unhappiness, but at least the prostitute lacks the housewife's hypocrisy, and the prostitute is not bound to the home or to one man. Yet both ways one is ultimately defeated. When this sort of world view is espoused by Georgie May, it may be considered plausible to her unfortunate condition; but her view also seems to be Bodenheim's. Life as a square has its banalities and limitations, but such a life does not obligatorily lead directly to the vast depression Georgie finds herself in when temporarily a bourgeois housewife.

She rightly sees the brutality, the bickering, the attritive tedium of life lived above the moral level of the streets. But, when Bodenheim indicates that this is all there is to see, his view seems crippled, oversimplified. Bodenheim produces finally melodrama —good melodrama—but not anything approaching a complex, tragic view of life. Georgie's embracing of defeat may stem from a near-tragic revelation, but Bodenheim's insistence upon the necessity and rightness of her suicide is only sad.

II Sixty Seconds (1929)

Sixty Seconds reveals Bodenheim's dissatisfaction with the technically old-fashioned novel form he had regularly employed. For example, the book uses a sometimes double time frame to focus on his protagonist's reminiscences. Thematically, the book is standard, for its hero, John Musselman, is another young city dweller rebelling from restrictive parents and environment. As in *Blackguard* and in *Crazy Man*, the central character is a criminal; he is in jail awaiting execution. In each of four sections Musselman looks out his cell window or around his narrow room and sees something that reminds him of earlier times. Each memory concerns a woman, and each woman helps define a stage in his education. First, Musselman looks at the sky, which reminds him of when he was eighteen in Chicago, walking along the rails. As the eighteen-year-old Musselman walks, he in turn remembers his initiation in sex, and the next twenty pages chronicle this initiation. Then the double flashback fades, and Bodenheim returns to the single flashback of Musselman mooning along the railroad tracks. He looks up from his reveries to see a young girl being attacked by dogs, and he chases and kills a dog. Then for over a hundred pages Bodenheim narrates John's affair with this girl, arranging the events chronologically. The now single flashback proceeds to where the girl, Elizabeth, departs. John decides to " 'bo" it on the road since the octoroon Elizabeth has been taken away from him by her parents. The section concludes with the condemned man still looking out his cell window, watching a robin. Ten seconds have passed since he saw the sky.

Bodenheim's use of time is related to Henri Bergson's *durée*, which explores intense units of non-clock time where each second or minute can be packed with vital experience. For Musselman, time is psychologic not chronologic. He relives two crucial experiences within ten seconds, but the experiences themselves took many months to develop. The first sentences of *Sixty Seconds* focus on time: "Oh let us leave metaphysical conjectures for a time. It may be indeed that Time is one of the dimensions in space. If a man could stand far apart from the earth, and if the light from his eyes could travel toward the earth quintillions of times faster than that light which makes our days and nights, then this man might be able to watch events that happened on the earth three or four hundred years ago."

Later, when John Musselman's eyes see no longer his youth but his cell window—and Bodenheim seems to agree with Wordsworth that as we age "Shades of the prisonhouse begin to close/ Upon the growing boy"—the reader learns that another ten of his lifetime of sixty seconds have passed. Then Bodenheim restates his concept of *durée*: "Ten seconds have flown by—seconds of remembrance so quick and searing that hours shrank to fractions within them." He further comments with a poeticized combination of Bergson and of the concept of entropy: "Time is only the inevitable dream with which motion of every kind assumes the attributes of advancing and perishing, and if all things were to stand forever still, time would disappear." Then a robin lights on the window sill, and past and present again intermingle. For John, the motion of the mind itself is time, not the motion of the clock. Bodenheim here reaffirms what he had stated nine years previously in "Advice to a Pool": "Time is but the phantom dagger/ That motion lifts to slay itself."

Playing with time is not the only way Bodenheim experiments in *Sixty Seconds*. A family squabble is reported in play form, complete with stage directions. This technique is not new—F. Scott Fitzgerald did it in *The Beautiful and Damned* (1922), for instance—but it is new to Bodenheim. Though his reporting of speech and action is faithful, he calls attention to his trick by concluding the playlet with "and now, the stenographer has dropped his pencil, having reproduced the exact words that the prototypes of his men and women have uttered. . . . A trivial achievement, but one worshiped by the 'critics' of our country and time." Later he reports the emotions of Elizabeth in a free-verse poem of over fifty lines.

Still later Bodenheim interrupts his narrative with "At this point, the mingling of narrative, essay, and poem will become suggestive and disorganized for the time being, to avoid the host of descriptive and analytical details which so many people relish but which are distasteful to the present writer." Then follows a highly impressionistic section comprised of scraps of dialogue, various characters' random thoughts, miscellaneous descriptions, and what must be Bodenheim philosophizing. The experiment does not work, but not because Bodenheim is trying something new; the writing is simply bad. Yet he was determined to avoid writing a Realistic novel and so, in one way or another, he frequently reminds his reader that what he is reading *is* a novel, in much the same way that Ionesco reminds the theatergoer that he is watching a play, not reality. Some of Bodenheim's experimentation seems cinematic: flashbacks were a favorite movie device, as demonstrated by D. W. Griffiths' *Intolerance*. He also included in the text what he footnotes as "a case-history from an actual dance-hall girl in Chicago." The case history is realistically written in the idiom of its speaker, and it provides a number of details demonstrating the sordid existence that city life spawns. When John finally explodes into murder, the tensions within him and the pressures exerted on him directly relate to the sexually sick world the dance-hall girl describes.

Despite the experimentation, Musselman's life is the novel's focal point. He is another of Bodenheim's wounded misfits, a brave rebel against all authority. Through most of the novel Musselman rebels through escape. He wanders on the road from Chicago to the Southwest, bums around Texas, picks cotton, and finally bobs to the surface in New York. His departures are not caused purely by the economic necessity moving Dos Passos' "Vag" or Jack Conroy's *Disinherited*: Musselman is an underdog more from choice than from necessity, but he seeks no beatific Nirvana. He is close to that contemporary hero, the "saint, dreamer, and maniac" whose danger to society proves society's corruption, a lay Christ martyred by Middletown. Bodenheim emphasizes Christ imagery throughout John's portrayal. "Nails in the boards continually" jab John's hands as he helps demolish an old hotel. He hops a freight to "Libertyville, Texas," and is immediately forced to pick cotton or go to jail. Picking cotton, he digs his own "nails into [his] flesh." He is born on a Good Friday and dies about the same age as Christ died, when he is thirty-two or thirty-three. He even temporarily saves a Mary Magdalene, a taxi-dancer and prostitute.

But Musselman is a contemporary Christ whose sacrifice is gratuitous since it leads neither to individual purgation nor to recognition by the community. When John finally stops running and kills the woman who has irresponsibly tempted him, he places himself in the maw of society. John's murder by society duplicates civilization's greater crimes—wars, slow starvation of the poor, the general mutilation of mind and body by vicious contemporary life, murdering of reputation by newspapers, killing youths' "normal lust for each other's bodies." But John's own confrontation with the enemy leads only to his miserable destruction. Society does not recognize his sacrifice: his rebellion is ineffective. As Richard Lehan writes of the modern Existential hero, John "does not reaffirm his identity through a tragic fall. Rather his tragic quest usually allows no noble form of self-fulfilment or higher return to the community, and often leads to a form of self-destruction."[2]

The particular social enemies in *Sixty Seconds* are clear enough. But Bodenheim muddles together his own antagonists with his hero's. Bodenheim attacks Humanist critics, literary critics in general, organized religion, the city, parents, restrictive morality, school, God, and *The New Yorker*. Negro sex is commended, for Negroes "have less shame in them and they was more honest." Youth (with a capital "Y") is praised, if it is free and liberated. We are pressed to develop sympathy for "tragically valiant . . . Youth" because it must wear brassieres "to keep the breasts from bobbing a little with the walking of legs."

Bodenheim is more successful in describing details relevant to the book's central action. He delineates the young, tentative romance of John and Elizabeth convincingly, and he well portrays John's doubts, his attraction and repulsion upon learning that Elizabeth is part Negro. While John honestly loves Elizabeth, knowing she is part Negro, he has sexual intercourse with her only after discovering her Negro blood. He has previously slept with white girls, but only those he considered loose. Thus he displays vestiges of white folklore concerning the morality of Negroes. Bodenheim also fills the book with small well-observed details such as John's suitably adolescent description of Elizabeth's mouth as "hot ice-cream."

Bodenheim also continues his attack on urban squalor. Throughout the book, the city is shown as a prime agent of ugliness and destruction of humanity. John and Elizabeth grow freely and innocently in love in a park area, or where open fields remove them from the city's crush and filth. But when they move from the "wind-tossed, madrigaled freedom of flowers, weeds, and the unconcerned shadows of a tree" to the city with its red-brick apartments, garbage cans, rusty screen doors, fly-specked windows, their innocence is hit by "hard, what-have-you-been-up-to looks." While John walks with Elizabeth along the city streets, he first hears "Bo-oy, you're picking 'em dark this season, ain't you?" and "here, niggy, niggy, niggy" from the white boys who have already unsuccessfully sought Elizabeth out: "she might be a shine, but dogone if she didn't look mighty like a white girl— two pleasures rolled into one."

As always, Bodenheim fleshes out his basic narrative with philosophic asides. His generalizations do not attack the heart of his real enemy but rather prick a child's balloon he has himself blown up. When he shouts against the "spurious mystics" who "almost two thousand years ago" pronounced the "clean, powerful, springy flesh of human being . . . unclean and evil," one wonders precisely whom he is talking about. These same "mystics . . . manufactured" the words "sin" and "sinful." Bodenheim sees the antagonist in terms of a handy cartoon figure, like the spirit of prohibition so frequently portrayed in the 1920's. Such pseudo-philosophizing obscures more about the nature of man than it reveals.

And the book has other shortcomings. More clumsy sentences exist than should at this stage of Bodenheim's development. Once he writes: "when hair is clipped from a head, an essential sincerity shows itself openly on this head." His running battle with the critics is irrevelant. His interpolated veracity is questionable; he says: "once I saw a college Dean of Sociology turn to a berserk creature when some one called him a god-damn bastard." And he repeats an earlier fault in permitting his characters to think sometimes in terms they clearly would not have employed. He once interjects: "these precise adjectives did not emerge in his mind, but a wordless approach to them fought in his head." In *Georgie May* the omniscient author became an immediately concerned participant evoked by the horror of contemporary society. The unmistakable odor of what Bodenheim thought his personal failure permeates *Sixty Seconds*.

In John Musselman's life the reader observes the seeds of misery and finally its blossoming. He sees the bigotry and small-mindedness of everyday people in a hostile environment. He watches restrictive society warp and then finally break a man. Each agent of pressure—the parent, the neighborhood, the city, society—is observed in action. And the weaknesses in John are also detailed: unrealistic, a drifter, he invites trouble partly through his own ignorance. Bodenheim's experiments with presenting time effectively focus on crucial moments, and show John's development from a good kid to a cold killer without accumulating the trivial detail a more minute chronicle of his ten year's career would demand. The reader hears with John the soundless ticking away of those final sixty seconds, but almost as loud sounds Bodenheim's heard voice. He nearly dominates the book, and his troubles with the world and literary critics become far too important. The writer who was often a moralist had temporarily become an apologist.

III A Virtuous Girl *(1930)*

A Virtuous Girl employs essentially the same theme as *Sixty Seconds*: a youthful rebel frees herself from the oppressive morality of communal and parental authority. Emmy Lou Wilkins expresses her rebellion through complete sexual liberation. In sleeping with whomever she wants when she wants she achieves, if not happiness, then what seems in the novel even better—freedom. Emmy does not, like Jessica Maringold, become jaded or corrupted by her erotic adventures. She remains throughout the novel untainted, "a virtuous girl." Though a virgin at the book's start and sexually inexperienced, she already knows that sex is "bee-oo-ti-iful, oh so bee-o-oo-ti-iful, and warmly spiced"; and she wonders "dimly, in the chime-laden, palpitantly unequipped depths of her virginal heart . . . why people made it, oh, kind of ugly."

Bodenheim's thesis—that society's sex attitudes are foolish, that young erotic impulses are strong and basically healthy and should be permitted freer expression—is placed in a fictional context sometimes difficult to examine seriously. His failure casts doubt on his corollary thesis, that Emmy Lou can be a sexual cornucopia and remain virtuous. Bodenheim, who tells a good deal about Emmy's sexual beliefs, often agrees with them. But her thinking is too often ludicrous, and her actions are so tailored by Bodenheim to demonstrate the proof of her erotic philosophy that the pattern of her life emerges in gross and unrealistic over-simplification. We are simply told that Emmy's "heart was not carnal but fearlessly bird-like in the flutterings of a longing for . . . space-erasing, sweetly vowing sex." Emmy is described as unmoral but never coarsely lustful, promiscuous but choosy and always innocent. Her sexual behavior is so unrealistically stripped of probable concomitants that she is unbelievable in action. Half-pursuer, half-pursued, pulling her first lover down upon her, she appears utterly passionless and unheated, a merry little rebel.

Bodenheim is far more successful in creating a believable sense of place than in making Emmy Lou a believable character. The novel is filled with a nostalgically realistic portrayal of life in "the Good Years." Emmy Lou and Dick stand drinking magic and romantic soda pop while watching a parade, fingers locked together. Later, they sneak out to Frankel's ice-cream parlor with its Chinese lanterns and strings of paper daisies. "It's so ducky and plummy today, Dickie," she tells him. Life is filled with kid's games and snatches of kid's talk. "Here we come. Where from? Philadelphia. What's your trade? Lemonade. Give us some. . . . Shamey thing, shamey thing, wo-ouldn't te-ell hi-is mo—other—er." Hymns like "Nearer my God, To Thee" are sung as "Nero, my dog, has fleas." "Just break the news to mother" becomes "just break your snooze and stutter." The surface simplicity of life is fully rendered, and it is occasionally compared to what this life was giving way to. "Wait Till the Sun Shines, Nellie," Bodenheim says, is turning into "Red-Hot Mamma, Twist Your Red-Hot Lips with Me."

Emmy's romance with Dick is portrayed, until his seduction, with a light comic touch somehow suitable to the ice-cream parlor world they inhabit. Once when they are madly kissing, "their lips in a moist insanity of possessiveness," Bodenheim notes that tender passion must surrender to mosquito bites. "That was the only reason I stopped kissing you," Dick says, "a big one was just boring into my leg!" Yet Bodenheim does not simply present an unrelievedly pastoral existence; he recognizes the tawdriness and intellectual poverty displayed in the homey decor of the Wilkins' apartment with its "swivel piano-stool with four legs ending in glass balls," its "bust of Shakespeare and the statuette of 'Rebecca At the Well,'" its "Axminster carpet woven into brown and green hexagons, suggestions of flowers."

For the student of Bodenheim's life, the book is significant in the sometimes disguised and sometimes overt ways it uses Bodenheim's biography. Bodenheim predates the book by about eight years, but otherwise it follows many patterns and events of his life. Both Emmy and he rebelled from their parents; both left home at about seventeen; both appear to love the father but not the mother. Both had relatively strong, domineering mothers and less authoritarian fathers. Emmy rebelled through sex and Bodenheim through art, but in *A Virtuous Girl* he notes that Emmy's sexual impulses are merely diverted artistic ones.

As stated, the book's major theme is rebellion from authority, seemingly the major theme of Bodenheim's life. Dickie, the first lover, is discarded precisely because he does not rebel from his parents. The nearest approach Emmy has to a satisfactory and lasting love is with Elmer, who, like Emmy, had also run away from home. Like so many of Bodenheim's wandering characters, Emmy starts off on the road but quickly settles down to a new home; for Blanche in *Ninth Avenue* and Selma in *Crazy Man* do the same. This pattern reflects Bodenheim's own dual tendencies to find a home and then leave it. The search for satisfaction circles around inevitably to a new haven, which in turn becomes a prison to be escaped from. What becomes authority must be rebelled against. In *A Virtuous Girl* Emmy "just won't be roped down." She also dislikes the authoritarian policeman who makes "no distinction between actual criminals and people whose hearts wanted to be free." Emmy also knows that her job supervisor hates her, and is determined to keep her own private life beyond the boss's interference. She also rebels from kneeling "to be forgiven by God, or her parents"—a significant linking for both Emmy Lou and Bodenheim. As is true of many erotic relationships in Bodenheim's books, love or successful sex seems possible in *A Virtuous Girl* only when Emmy sees the partner as a baby or as a very young boy; she is always maternal to her lovers. Male figures, as in *Blackguard, Ninth Avenue,* or *Replenishing Jessica,* reveal themselves in the converse relationship; they are infants or boys to be mothered.

Several years after she has left her parents, Emmy returns home. Her father is dead and her mother blames her for his death. Here Bodenheim's guilt concerning his own rebellion is manifest; moreover, his father also died before his mother. In the book Emmy successfully defends herself against her mother's charges, and the novel concludes with Mrs. Wilkins *now forgiven by Emmy,* falling to her knees and sobbing against her daughter's bosom. How pleased Bodenheim must have felt at this scene. But he never achieved expiation in his own life, nor was he ever in a position with his mother to distribute forgiveness and mercy, though he surely must have wished to find himself in such a situation. He was rarely, if ever, able to forgive anyone.

The psychological insights the book provides on Bodenheim cannot increase its esthetic value. His premise that the very young lovers should be permitted "to hug each other openly, thoroughly, in full, sappy, crudely tossing beauty of daylight"—here "hug" represents the sex act—is not fully or realistically demonstrated. The complex ramifications of such a shift in morals are ignored.

Furthermore, too much of his moralizing is fuzzy and irrelevant. After Dick Rosenstein demonstrates his understandable ignorance of women, a separate paragraph blurts "O budding, ignorant sentimentality, so far removed from the one coined into dollars by shrewd panderers, and the treacle served by adult cowards, who employ it to soften their iron corsets—you have within you all of the unprotected sublimity held by one kind of youth." Later one learns in an interpolated aside that "life is an array of play-boys, play-girls, on one side, and actual artists on the other, with a mass of self-blind, slavish babblers in between— slaves of every kind, from communist to burgher, street-sweeper to king, strumpet to housewife."

The flaws in *A Virtuous Girl* are especially disappointing since the book begins so promisingly, and since it contains throughout much effective material. Apart from the sexual bravado forced upon her, Emmy Lou is an interesting turn-of-the-century girl, a rebellious miss caught in a period of transitional stress, both historically and personally. When she and her young friends flirt with sex, the book offers interesting and entertaining insights into adolescent behavior. Bodenheim's re-evoking of the time is often effective, for scraps of dialogue and snapshots of life as it was then lived illuminate much of the book. And Bodenheim continues to have a surer command of technique—when he keeps himself out of the book's texture. He employs extensively for the first time stream-of-consciousness, and he again handles flashback sequences competently. His description of those supposedly good years is filled with technically well-put-forth details of character and place. But, when he propagandizes, and does so shakily, the book is marred.

IV   Naked on Roller Skates (1930)

The versatile Bodenheim changed directions in his next book. The seriousness of his tone had increased steadily from his first book, *Blackguard,* and in *A Virtuous Girl* his philosophizing had become quite heavy-handed. As the title suggests, *Naked on Roller Skates* is not only one of Bodenheim's more sensational novels but also one of his most comic. The book is in fact comic to the degree that it is sensational in its parodying of young and old frantically searching for "kicks" in the last years of the Jazz Age. Bodenheim provides his readers with an extraordinary number of thrills in presenting a descent into the underworld by his life-tasting hero and heroine. He describes several bloody fights, near murders, the obligatory trip to a Harlem nightclub—no sensational New York novel would be complete without one—miscegenation, a fifty-six-year-old man being seduced by a seventeen-year-old girl he has just met, a sixteen-year-old blonde necking in a den of thieves with a forty-year-old man, near kidnapping, a crooked poker game exploding into a free-for-all, latent incest, gangsters, and a protection racket. In fact, Bodenheim reduces to absurdity the sensationalistic city novel of crime and sex.

Bodenheim once again employs as his hero a liberated male

who has wandered on the road experiencing life fully, but this time he is one capable of triumphing over all situations, no matter how difficult or dangerous. The hero, Terry Barberlit, is matched with a blundering young woman, Ruth Riatt, who wants to wallow in the mud of life just to see what doing so is like. As the novel proceeds, it grows increasingly apparent that Ruth really wants Terry and a wild but definite domesticity. While Bodenheim leaves himself room to philosophize over favorite themes within this comic and picaresque frame-work, he speaks sparingly. Certain weaknesses of *Sixty Seconds* and *A Virtuous Girl* are therefore minimized.

The book's title is a mixture of the comic and serious. "We're all naked on roller skates. Naked on roller skates and sliding down into nowhere. Nowhere"—reiterates the sense of doom and nothingness found in such books as Fitzgerald's *The Beautiful and Damned* and Hemingway's *The Sun Also Rises;* but Bodenheim's ludicrous phrasing ridicules the nothing concept. He fuses this ridicule in *Naked on Roller Skates* with a fantasy of violence and sex. The novel begins with Terry's entering a small town selling snake oil and advocating the same "calisthenics and sexual advice" as "Benito MacFooey" (Bernarr MacFadden, who once suggested as cancer treatment fasting, exercise, and a "vitality building regimen"). Terry blunders into a brutal knee-in-the-groin fight with the local gas-station attendant after he is called a "jazzbo" and replies that the attendant is "bohunk." Later, he bumps into seventeen-year-old Roberta, while going for a drink of water. Roberta "pawed at his shoulders . . . and strained against him . . . her breath exuding into him, like a spasmodic blast of heat." After they rut, young Roberta tells Terry he is "a peacherino."

Terry is himself one of the book's chief comic figures. A Bodenheimian *übermensch*, he is incredibly competent, so completely the master of any situation, that he cannot be taken seriously. He even refers to himself as a cross between Don Juan and a nincompoop. Moreover, his fantastic history is a Jungian journey through Everyman's Walter Mittyland. He has lived with bush natives in South Africa, fought with the Boers and received a near-fatal head wound, been "taken prisoner by the British and escaped by setting fire to the kraal" that imprisoned him, then crossed two hundred miles of veldt to the west shore. There he shipped to Shanghai where he killed a coolie, then fled to Singapore, beachcombed a while in Hawaii, joined an army of revolutionists in Mexico, fought for the British in World War I, and throughout his adventures wrote poetry. At any moment his mind is apt to slide into memories of "over three decades of seances with death in the trenches of Africa, Mexico, China: slugging matches with extinction in the dives of Shanghai, Colombo, and Buenos Aires: escapes from the jails of Tampico and South Africa: tank plunges in American circuses: ticklish scrapes in the . . . forts of Chicago, New York, Frisco, where he was known as 'The General.'" Selling his panacea, he suddenly thinks "what a comedown from the hard-riding, nerveless man who had faced Zapata in an arroyo and told him to take a flop for himself." And looking at Ruth walking next to him, he remembers "that love sally for the girl in Vera Cruz—Pequita. Steel and blood love, with murder and sainthood in every last breath of it. . . . Black infernos for eyes." Yet he is also a tender man, a gentle tough "like Wallace Berry," as Ruth thinks.

In sections of his other novels, the highly ornate baroque splendor of his phrasing works against Bodenheim, appearing incongruous and showy. But in Terry's world of comically heightened experiences Bodenheim's too ripely poetic rhetoric is fitting. Metaphors describing simple natural act and fact become self-enraptured artifacts: the sun's light filtering through clouds "sometimes raced down from their cylindric edges, like the birth of a poem fighting off the rain-threats of centuries"; a fat off-duty policeman and his paramour discuss a business deal and "between the heavy-money talk, they kissed like steam-shovellers behind in their work"; evening does not approach, rather "a pint of lavender-indigo twilight was being economized in the air"; one man is colored "a luscious lemon-cream, with a face as gorgeous as an indestructible petunia."

The last two quotations specifically parody the Ronald Firbanks lushness of Carl Van Vechten's exotic *Nigger Heaven*. Bodenheim also includes in his book several wonderfully obscure Negro slang dialogues and a glossary of terms, both of which are Van Vechten devices in *Nigger Heaven*. One dialogue starts: "I say you one them lippy-chasers." "You take you black." "What?"

"I say one them lippy chasers. . . ." "Take you bah-bah. . . ." "Take you three nine." "Three nine go stick it." The glossary is clearly needed. Bodenheim plays with his own style of description: a mechanic has a "saggy face with raggy lips"; Ruth is a "pugilistic sylph"; one woman is a "yellow hornbill in vermillion canton crepe, with a truncated hate on her face"; another is "a fulvous woman with a fungoid face." An "orchestra swerved into a waltz 'A Russian Lullaby'—in which a Slavic folksong was cremated and reduced to the memory of an audible protest."

Ruth and Terry wander through this comic and sensational world. Terry has already mastered life by accepting it and not succumbing to cynicism, by experiencing all that he can without expecting much. A throwback to the Yankee peddler of American folklore and fiction, Terry has lived through many occupations and places and sells his snake oil. Terry enters Ruth's drab village like a rainmaker and sweeps out hoping for something good with Ruth, yet not really expecting much. He is uncommitted to family, society, to any particular religion including atheism.

Ruth is a twenty-four-year-old discontent whose too-early marriage has left her physically and emotionally unsatisfied. She tells Terry, "I want an A number one, guaranteed bastard. . . . I want him to beat my heart and beat my brain. I want him to hurt me so I'll get wise. I . . . want to open up my heart and let the mud in." Yet it becomes increasingly apparent that, as she entices a Harlem nightclub owner, or permits herself to be seduced by a rough she is actually revulsed by, she really wants Terry to commit himself and declare his need for her.

Although basically comic, the book involves ideas Bodenheim considered serious. One important theme of the book is the contrast between town and city, and a related theme is the gradual disintegration of identifiable town life. The novel opens in the spring of 1928, in Katoonah, Connecticut, a village as opposed to a suburb, still not essentially connected to city life. Its style is slow, dull, generally unviolent, sex- and sensation-starved, though both sex and sensation lurk beneath its drab exterior. Village morality is restrictive. In his spiel to the villagers, Terry doesn't refer specifically to the kidneys because such reference might offend the small-town audience. Still, the citizens want to listen to his talk because it offers them entertainment, a chance to hear something a little different. Starved for drama, they enjoy the verbal contests Terry's talk occasions. "Rubbish" is on the old men's faces, "the flunkeyism of centuries." But the young men are "still sexually vibrant, still had a fighting zip to their fists, still looked forward to a foxtrot, a velvety vamp of a girl."

In the city, life demands a quicker pace, and cutthroat competition in business and personal relationships. Sex is more open, but also more perverse. Villagers may be yokels, but most city dwellers that Ruth and Terry meet are "sharps" or thieves. The village old are marked by toil and denial: one is a "middle-aged woman garroted unawares by elderliness in her fortieth year with a jack-o-lantern face in which the candle was sputtering out." But the city creates its special effects too: "Poor Diana, trying to be a crook, and a good pal, and a miser, and a philanthropist, with each one completely unaware of the other, because the virus of the city had made her sixty-four when she should have been thirty-two."

Whatever bucolic placidity the village offers—and Bodenheim shows a short-tempered, reluctant fondness for its ways—is passing. Both Terry, who was born in a small Midwestern town, and Ruth, reared "in a New Hampshire Village—a nook where salacity and the Congregationalist Church broke each other's hearts to no avail," leave the village for New York, then leave—Ruth with bullet wound—for Chicago. Main Street's elms and hollyhocks are clearly losing the battle to "bright red gasoline pumps" and "Coke" posters blossoming along its now macadamized paths. Mechanization, World War I, and the car all contribute to the time when "shy feminine innocence would soon be a relic." Bodenheim notes that small-town flappers are becoming as pseudo-sophisticated as their city counterparts.

Bodenheim shows in *Naked On Roller Skates,* as he did in *Georgie May* and *A Virtuous Girl,* that American life shifts so rapidly that traditions beyond the ersatz are almost impossible to establish. This difficulty exists in village or city life. He describes one village parlor and one Harlem parlor to symbolize this not-so-comic absence of valuable tradition. In the village room are "a conglomeration of Mission furniture: colonial antiques; rag rugs; a grandfather clock; and old, upright piano; the inevitable radio-set. . . . a conch-shell with a kewpie on it: a Mutt and Jeff comicstrip framed . . . a chain of paper forget-me-nots: a slim French made doll." In the Lenox Avenue "cage" are a "jumble of fake mahogany and gorgeously enamelled pine. . . . purple leather divan . . . wax tulips in a Bohemian glass vase . . . handpainted chinaware on lace-linen spreads. . . . A tuba in a black case standing on a sacred pile of *Breezy Stories*." Terry's and Ruth's furniture is "wicker, Japanese, and Turkish thrown together." In such a shifting society, the clutter and detritus of cheap fashion are often the only maintainable tradition.

Basically a simple, exuberant work, *Naked on Roller Skates* makes many of its points more tellingly than some of Bodenheim's more portentous and pretentious fictions. The book is comic, but says that the darker side of life must be experienced, that the individual must liberate himself from society's foolish restraints. It attacks the mechanized drabness of comtemporary life and the magnetic viciousness of the city. Bodenheim preaches less and relates his style to his matter: the romantic posturings of his freed superman are matched by Bodenheim's comic prose. "Hey, big boy," Ruth says, "put the brakes on for a minute. You'll be skidding into the furniture. You're speeding on a wet road, big boy." Terry answers "Speeding hell, I'll be stalled on the turnpike if I don't get better service at this filling station." Though certain crudities of phrasing and technique are not parodies or burlesques but simply bad writing, the book remains a comic success and shows once more that Bodenheim was at his best when sticking in sight of reality. He had an eye for the significant detail or turn of speech, and the ability to re-create what he saw and heard.

V Bringing Jazz! *(1930)*

If *Naked on Roller Skates* is Bodenheim's most free-wheeling fiction, *Bringing Jazz!* is his most exuberant book of poems. Published in 1930, it belongs more to the wild decade Bodenheim had just lived through, the 1920's, than to the sad one he approached. The book is difficult to evaluate, since its poems vary from comic doggerel to jazz lyrics for as yet unwritten melodies, to impressionistic jazz tone poems. Bodenheim prefaced the poems by saying that "these poems were written to be set to music, and a jazz composer is earnestly invited," but not many of the individual works can be treated as potential lyrics for songs. Some could only with difficulty be accompanied by a subordinate jazz background, while others, such as the title poem, would make very good jazz entertainment pieces for poetry and jazz readings.[3] Bodenheim uses the term "jazz" loosely, seeming to suggest by it "low down" music and lyrics, highly colloquial diction, frequent and playful rhymes, but not any well-defined technical or rhythmic mode. He does not distinguish consistently between "blues," Dixieland (with all its varieties), rag time, Mickey Mouse, syncopated dance band, or other specific subcategories of jazz. He uses the term broadly, producing a kind of "pop"-art poetry. That the book lacks philosophic depth and artistic intensity is perhaps inherent in the nature of his limited concept of popular poetry.

Bodenheim's efforts to employ jazz ranged from the slight to the great in *Bringing Jazz!* "Greenwich Village Jazz I" is primarily a comic description of various characters and the lives they lead in the Village, somewhat like John Reed's privately printed (1913) "The Day in Bohemia." Both poems employ what could be called journalistic Broadway jazz. Bodenheim's work demands heavy footnoting now, and the footnoting tramples much of the poem's humor. But many of the comic lines and rhymes are enjoyable with a minimal knowledge of allusions. The poem's opening, "The weather is fine in Montana—/ Though afternoons sometimes get hot," refers specifically to Eli Siegal, whose notorious prize-winning "Hot Afternoons There Are in Montana" Bodenheim parodies. "A playwright from Broadway,/ Who once was a newspaper bird./ When he starts to converse in an awed way,/ No one near him can get in a word!" could satirize mildly any number of loquacious authors, including Ben Hecht. A "millionaire-poet who's wise!—" is clearly Robert Clairmont, Bodenheim's friend from the Greta Garbo Club. By the time the poem was published, poor Clairmont was no longer a millionaire nor wise. Today, types rather than individuals are recognizable and amusing in the poem. We still have "Village Poet Two-Forty,/ Who sings of a pale, Chinese moon./ His appearance is rugged and sporty,/ And somehow it conflicts with his tune." And who has not seen or heard of the lady of "twenty,/ With spangles and angles of arms./ She recites dripping verses with plenty/ Of remarks on her spasmodic charms."

"Underworld Jazz II" mocks the literary-cinematic projection of the criminal world. In this jazzy rather than jazz poem, Bodenheim crams together the plots of hard-boiled novels and films with what passed for crook's dialogue in these works to create a comic impression of Ben Hecht's and W. R. Burnett's province. "Crack!—another revolver—Little Napoleon killed his fifteenth man./ Whack! He tried hard to solve her,/ But when he failed he had to smack her pan./ 'Say . . . we'll slip him the leather'—/ Freddy the Goat could sling a nasty slang./ He . . . was wondering whether/ He could survive unless he killed his gang."[4] Bodenheim also satirizes the false sentimentality of the popular criminal: "Tennessee Ted knocks hoboes left and right./ Then . . . this noble deceiver/ Gives up his life to keep a maiden white." Bodenheim concludes that this world isn't real; "And you couldn't say that it was fantasy," just a lot of "Bang . . . Crash . . . Zowie . . . Groans" in the lowbrow marketplace.

Bodenheim narrowly escapes presenting this pseudo-world himself in "Underworld Jazz" I and III. "Underworld I" is a jazz poem patterned after "Frankie and Johnny," offering the story of Zelda and Danny. Bodenheim's reworking unfortunately lacks the haunting impact of the earlier song. His lyrics lack crude, direct simplicity; and his form employs no balladic refrain. Replacing "Oh lordy how they could love" is "Danny loved her quiet line/ When his hands became too rough./ Wouldn't squawk and couldn't whine—/ She was made of sterling stuff." "Sterling" strikes an especially artificial note. And where "Frankie and Johnny" uses simple, meaningful description, such as Johnny walking "in his bran' new hundred dollar suit," Bodenheim writes of "Green eyes like a torn-up frond/ Fallen from a rustic soul." In some ways Bodenheim only updates his version, replacing the original's bartender-squealer with a busybody columnist he calls "Wallace Ginsmell" in obvious allusion to Walter Winchell.

"Underworld III" chronicles the life and demise of Louie, "an East Side rat" with a mind like a "nickel gat." Louie's heart is cold except toward his little son. Louie is gunned down by other rats and dies after saving the son's life. The sentiment and melodrama in this lamentable history are staples of mass media which Bodenheim is here echoing but not parodying. As jazz lyric, the poem needs simplicity and directness. Bodenheim's more sophisticated metaphors are often interesting and arresting, however, as when he describes the son's resemblance to his father's "own thick lips/ Caught below a pair of eyes like frozen whips." In the same section, Louie's description tiptoeing to see his boy "like a chastised mouse" is obtrusively un-jazzlike. The story of the poem —Louie as a jazz gangster—is handled more successfully than the story's diction. Louie would be to the popular mentality a jazz-world crook, but the language is not often enough jazz-world lyrics.

Bodenheim is more successful when he can fuse his fanciful images with a vehicle demanding less simplicity and permitting greater jazz ecstasy. "Futuristic Jazz" begins "Smilax music . . . high C buds/ Climbing up from where the big drum thuds,/ Climbing into . . . flapper's souls,/ Twining life around the sleepy doles." The images then take off as in a jazz riff, portraying to the implicit beat of an incantatory drum the drunken, wild release of cheap dance-hall glories: "Whiskey music . . . spilled from flutes,/ Making drunkards out of sober youths." Bodenheim proceeds at this high pitch with a series of meaningful-meaningless images whose sexuality and rhythmic pattern parallel the "hambone-hambone" song and lyrics well known to Negro children and jazz musicians: "Mary's legs have . . . lost their bones,/ Now they're nothing but a French-horn's groans./ Mary's breasts have . . . lost their skin—/ Opened up to let a bass drum in/ . . . Mary's lips are . . . curving out—/ Found a saxaphone and lost their pout./ Mary's dress is . . . falling down—/ Soul's too light to wear a heavy gown." Bodenheim concludes with two final couplets slowing down the poem's pace and ending in a monosyllabic jazz *retardo* making sense from nonsense: "God-bye morals . . . so long fears—/ Everybody's crazy when the music leers./ Even Mother Grundy grins,/ Lifts her dress an inch and turns the safety pins!" Bodenheim underscores the *retardo* by noting that the reader is to read the last line slowly.

Jazz frenzy is also interestingly portrayed in "Jazz Kaleidoscope," a poem whose title indicates its shifting subject matter and variant jazz beats. Generally concerned with Negro life, the poem begins with a slowly insistent almost "boogie" beat: "It takes a good, old-fashioned midnight hell/ To make a dark man twist his hips. . . ./ You need a dark brown sister stepping wild,/ You need a dark brown stack of joy." Then terse lines reflect the excited shots of a crap game: "Bones, roll on that floor./ Bones, make it once more!/ Bones, seven's my score—/ My sugar needs a diamond ring./ Bones, here's where we ride,/ Bones, come on and slide./ Bones, keep on my side—/ I've got to make my sugar sing." Bodenheim ends this section, whose rhythm and diction throughout are natural echoes of a crap game, with another *retardo* (a marginal note explains "last line slow"), "I need just one more black-eyed eight!"

The next section employs the slow, sensuous beat of the "blues" melodic line. The language is that of a dirty "blues." "Oh Mamie Lou, you're squeezing/ Blood roses . . . in my breast,/ Blood-moanings . . . and teasing/ Blood-whispers . . . I can't rest!/ Oh Mamie Lou, your eyes are/ Black panthers . . . in soft dens." Other jazz patterns employed include a section that Bodenheim notes is "somewhat connected with 'The Memphis Blues,'" a section whose metrical pattern parallels that of the well-known "Down in Alabamy," though Bodenheim does not point this out: "Listen you palm-scratchers,/ Lippy baby-snatchers—/ Stay way from mah Harlem chippy, 'less ah get mad!" The truly kaleidoscopic shots of Negro low life which began with sex end with death. Another "hambone" passage sings a lament for a dead Negro: "Some white driftah jumped a chile. . . ./ Cain't ketch him so we's to bile. . . . Sing it sad and sing it low:/ They dragged mah boy out fum dat day./ Struck him down and burned him slow,/ But we'll get even some sweet day."

Other jazz ballads employ a quick ricky-tic beat and Tin-Pan-Alley rhymes for comic purposes. Among these are "Bronx Jazz I," a tale of unfortunate love in the city: "Tessie Goldberg had a smile like dollars/ In love with scholars/ In starched white collars/ And silk shirts. . . . /Tessie fell for dilletantes and glib men/ Who spoke of Ibsen/ And rhymed their fibs when/ They saw skirts." "Bronx Jazz II" counsels its heroine Sophie: "When your Auntie—/ Raves in G andante, —/ Snicker when her tones grate:/ 'Dun't get back late!'"

Two of the most effective poems in *Bringing Jazz!* show what is probably the major non-musical influence on Bodenheim's jazz works, the poems of Vachel Lindsay. Neither "Street-Level Jazz" nor "Bringing Jazz" employs Lindsay-like orchestral directions, as do several of Bodenheim's other poems. But both echo the supposedly primitive rhythm of the bass sections in I and II of "The Congo" and in the loud bass sections in I and II of "General William Booth Enters Into Heaven." Lindsay's "Fat black bucks in a wine-barrel room" and "Booth led boldly with his big bass drum" foreshadow the opening of "Street-Level Jazz": "Eighteen nickels and a rusty old dime." The Negro card-game violence portrayed in "Street-Level Jazz" is thematically similar to the world of the "Wild crap-shooters" in Lindsay's poem. All four poems employ the diction and rhythms of what could be called ecstatic evangelistic jazz: the "Hallelujah! It was queer to see/ Bull-necked convicts with that land make free" of "General William Booth"; or "The box-car gloried in its mirth—/ Just a hallelujah and a dancing thud./ And one old man opened up his shirt" in "Bringing Jazz."

In "Street-Level Jazz," Bodenheim alternates his heavy-beat lines with the more rapid shuffle rhythm of the drummer's whisk: "Eighteen nickels and a gallon of booze/ Bury Papa's heart-beats in a soft black ooze." In this way he suggests lyric line and afterthought amplification. In the last eight lines of the poem he shifts into a "blues" line with "I've got the dark, stark, long-nailed blues:/ I've got an old black-screaming mood." The more formal imagery of this "blues" section also shifts from the patter of the earlier "Listen, babe, I've got to fly southeast/ Nothing on and happy on a cake of yeast! .../ Fret my bones—you're bluffing on ace-high?/ Take your old bandana out and start to cry." In the "blues" section, Bodenheim uses the traditional image of escape and death, the railroad, to conclude the card game and its accompanying sexual byplay: "I'll take a long, deep, rasping breath/ And walk right down those railroad-ties." Thus by jazz rhythms, colloquial and specifically jazz diction, Bodenheim tells the story of a card-playing Negro, high on dope (yeast) at the beginning of the poem, but depressed and lamenting by the end of the game.

Since jazz probably began as a Negro expression of grief and happiness, it is only natural that many of the poems in *Bringing Jazz!* concern Negroes. But the book's title poem extends the jazz lament into areas more general and culturally more ominous.

This new lament belongs to no one man nor to Negroes, but to a whole generation of Depression bums riding the rods leading only to hobo jungles and nowhere. In many of the book's other poems jazz is part of a euphoric escape mechanism coupled with sex and alcohol: here it becomes frenzied violence in itself, a wild, destructive dance of death. To communicate all this, Bodenheim uses images of violence and oppression and crazed escape in lines alternately slow and quick, involving jangling internal, feminine, and masculine rhyme. The poem's first four lines are germinal, describing in honky-tonk rhythms a mad gathering of train-riding bums who try deadening oppression through jazz: "Last night I had an oboe dream—/ Whistlers in a box-car madness bringing jazz./ Their faces storm in a hobo-gleam,/ Blinding all the grinding wheels and singing jazz."

The lines continue relentlessly in obsessive, compulsive beat, showing a jungle tangle of men gone almost mad and on the road now, seeking apocalyptic liberation through jazz, seeking through disorder to burn away their grinding pain and maybe bring about order through controlled chaos: "The hoboes sang with scorching notes/ Burning up their pain into a gale of jazz,/ While sadness poured in their shaking throats,/ Like a molten bugle in a wail of jazz./ The rails were jails for death and rust—/ Holding up the cruel dark blue speed of jazz." Jazz is not now just music nor mere anodyne, but macabre jiggling on the edge of a doom both personal and historic: the year is 1930 for Bodenheim and the country. Finally, music comes "flaring and profound," permitting a nightmare vision of the jazz dance's ultimate and grotesque jig-steps: "And then I saw the dream's dark spring—/ Hurricanes of jazz born from the bottom-world./ 'Saint Louie Gal with a diamond ring'/ Danced with mobs of hoboes while the thunder swirled!" The bottom-dogs of sadness and deprivation and confusion join each other.

Bringing Jazz! is more than a noble endeavor. While not a collection of invariably first-rate poems of high seriousness, the volume uses jazz idiom and rhythms effectively and with freshness. Though Bodenheim reveals only an interested layman's understanding of a complex and various form, those jazz subjects, rhythms, and images that he employs are often used skillfully, and could have invigorated his poetry of the 1930's. From the comic jazz of "Greenwich Village" to the troubling sound of "Bringing Jazz," the book shows accomplishment in combining popular and high art. But it was an area he did not again explore with exuberance.

CHAPTER 5

Poet with His Lips Sealed

BODENHEIM'S pursuit of oblivion dragged slowly through the 1930's. For a time his troubles were minor. Edward Dahlberg remembers in *Alms for Oblivion* the period as one when the Bodenheims and Samuel Putnam and he visited at the Horace Gregorys: "At this time, unable to make money out of his verse, Bodenheim had devised a scheme for writing saleable novels for telephone operators, typists, and factory girls." Dahlberg also remembers the time that Solbert Bodenheim had to endure in his Ethical Culture school taunting children who whittled their fingers to shame him, crying "naked on roller skates! naked on roller skates!"

The profits from his last novels permitted another, and final trip to Europe, Bodenheim's last fling as a writer of recognized stature. Afterwards, he lived an increasingly underground existence until his murder in 1954. According to Samuel Putnam's *Paris Was Our Mistress*, Bodenheim cut a madcap figure in that city. He appeared constantly in a dinner coat, and he ran about town with a high diver whose English was limited to "you are very nice" and "I think that is lofty." Putnam also reported such memorabilia as that Bodenheim was squirted with seltzer by notorious, wonderful Kiki at the Quatz Arts Ball: thus Bodenheim blithely flung roses in not yet impoverished Babylon.

But Putnam's account omits that Bodenheim was accepted by the expatriate fraternity in Paris as an equal. Ezra Pound invited him to a special luncheon, more or less in his honor, which was held upstairs at the Restaurant de l'Odeon. Among the Bodenheim papers exists a sad reminder of that last happy time for the soon-to-be displaced author, the menu of that luncheon dated "May, 1930." Scrawled across the menu reads the legend "Sworn and attested to in a moment of heavenly sobriety by Maxwell

Bodenheim. We the undersigned certify Max Bodenheim was chaste, sober, and industrious, and [?] 2 hours in company of undersigned without Inebriety and [?] completely loving company [signed] Ford Madox Ford, Riva Putnam, Olga Rudge, Ezra Pround." And in Paris he wrote some prose sketches never published, and he shivered "at the idea of ever returning to a place as barbaric, raw, stridently shallow, mean, and uncouthly frenzied as New York" in "the land of Patriotism, Freedom, and wortleberries." But he returned late in the year to Depression America.

Bodenheim continued to write novels during the early 1930's, but none met critical or popular approval. *Duke Herring* in 1931 attempted to repay Hecht for *Count Bruga*, which was ostensibly inspired by various lies, legends, and facts of Bodenheim's life. Such a silly quarrel seemed petty and tasteless in a land of bread lines and apple carts. *Run, Sheep, Run* (1932) and *Slow Vision* (1934) both tried confronting the contemporary morass, but the radicalism of both is filled with so much hedging, the view of modern life so depressing, the eventual solution so far-off and tentative, that neither could have much success with public or critics. Even Bodenheim's temporary alignment with radical policy, when he attacked the National Recovery Act in *Slow Vision*, was soon undermined by the shifting policies of the People's Front. And he published no book of poetry from *Bringing Jazz!* in 1930 to *Lights in the Valley* in 1942: *Run, Sheep, Run* was dedicated "to a poet with his lips sealed."

I Duke Herring *(1931)*

Before composing his final novels of social consciousness, Bodenheim published his thinly disguised satiric attack on Ben Hecht, *Duke Herring*. The Depression had not yet awakened his political inclinations enough for him to forgo retaliating to Hecht's *Count Bruga* (1926). *Duke Herring* is Bodenheim's only completely comic novel. As such, it contains several effectively humorous situations and an acid portrait of Hecht. But the personal jest pales occasionally. The book does not offer enough overall comic detail that is independent of the Hecht-Bodenheim squabble, nor is the satire applicable enough to the general follies of mankind to have much pervasive relevance. The Duke is shown a ridiculous figure, and the caricature of Hecht must have satisfied Bodenheim, for it cuts deep. The question of the novel's success perhaps rests on whether Hecht was worth demolishing. Bodenheim performed a good hatchet job, but maybe on a cigar-store Indian.

Duke Arturo Herring's literary life centers about the proposed publication of a "moderately salacious" novel to be written by Herring and sold in a private, illustrated edition for ten dollars a copy. Herring wants two thousand dollars for the book in advance royalties, payable immediately; 40 per cent of the net profits; complete movie and stage rights; 50 per cent royalty on translations and foreign publication; and the illustrator paid separately, not from his royalties. He says his claims are "remarkably reasonable."

More space is afforded Herring's love life, or rather lack of love life. He is married; but, whenever he can, he cheats on his wife. He cannot do so often. His one supposed conquest is Alice Gusman, whose pleasure with him is "the pleasure of gripping a confirmed charlatan with an even stronger charlatanism of her own." Herring is otherwise a public Don Juan with privately no place to go but home or the local bagnio. The Duke's ineptness is well shown when he goes to the apartment of a local prostitute and half-impresses, half-amuses the resident whores. "Poor vacant child," he tells one girl, "tears are nestling in the depths of your ribaldry." Led on by cries of "speech! speech! Give mamma some big, red-hot ideas," Duke responds with more second-rate philosophizing: "Man's choice is always between strength and weakness, between the ego and the squirmings of a cripple." A whore interrupts "you're going to pay for this bath-robe if you keep on tearing it." Another says, "I could have sworn you was talking Polish." After more speeches, shirt and robe rippings, and a lull when Herring lights "a cigarette with the boredom of a Buddha forced into an illusion of motion," havoc erupts. Herring's prostitute decides that his money doesn't compensate for her revulsion, and she screams "get out of here." When the tattered Herring stands foolishly in her doorway trying to sneer, she kicks Herring in the shins and finally forces him out. He departs "with more speed than impressiveness, the amused invitation to a sneer still twitching indomitably between his lips and his long, pointed nose." But, walking along the street, his bones aching and head throbbing, he thinks: "An amusing night. He had caused an ordinary wench to fall into rabies of jealousy and utterly ignore her mercenary rites—a jovial phenomenon of its kind." He smiles complacently as he rides home in a Yellow Cab.

Ultimately, his wife discovers his affair with Alice and his invariably unsuccessful lechery. To Duke's chagrin, his wife divorces him. At heart he is a Babbitt, recoiling "from the idea of deserting the respectable safeguards and emoluments of his life, behind which he retained the ability to caper and imbibe without anxiety." Now the fake Don is hooked by mistress Alice. The novel's ending chills, for Herring is seen realizing he is trapped by his own false image, forced to whirl with Alice somewhat like Paolo and Francesca in the stifling wind of their dry lust. Alice presents him with a mirror image of his own cynicism, surrounding their life with fake intellectuals, "dawdlers and sycophants." Herring sits outside the drawing room where phonies have gathered to talk louder than Bach's "Sonata in G Minor." He hears Alice say "That was a boring piece. It reminds me of a child's finger exercise trying to be subtle." Her tones are Herring's. She is told: "But my dear, that was a sonata by Bach." Her voice rises again after a pause, strident and triumphant: "I might have known it. Of course. Haven't I always told you that Bach was lousy?" Herring "shivered, rid himself of an involuntary frown, and strode into the room." Here, at the end of the book, facing his comic and terrible fate, Herring achieves some depth of character.

But too much of the book is devoted to private jokes and personal matters. When Bodenheim writes of Herring that "tomorrow he would return to his thousand-and-one poses," the reader unfamiliar with Hecht's *Thousand and One Afternoons in Chicago* misses the jest. Naturally, the satirist demands a certain background of knowledge from his reader; but Hecht's character, at least in Bodenheim's hands, does not always seem capable of supporting major and significant satire, and so some demands are unjustified.

II Run, Sheep, Run *(1932)*

After *Duke Herring,* only incidental portions of his novels are comic. The country was of course in the midst of the Depression, and Bodenheim was having personal difficulties, artistic and otherwise. *Run, Sheep, Run* is his first radical novel. The book develops three of the four basic areas Walter Rideout claims are the essential categories of the American radical novel. The work documents an individual's increasing knowledge of class-consciousness; deals in part with the life of "bottom dogs," the lowest layers of society; and portrays middle-class decadence. *Run, Sheep, Run* does not describe a strike (the fourth category), though it does report anti-state riots. Part of Bodenheim's point in the book is that the oppressed workers who should be striking are not yet aware of this beginning solution to their troubles or, if aware, are incapable of instigating agitation.

The book's hero George Romaine, an admitted Communist, searches for an effective plan of behavior in an economically and morally corrupt society. Surrounding him are various people representing degrees of partial commitment, insensitivity, blindness, and brutal antagonism. George first wanders through the world of New York middle-class intellectuals, fellow travellers, and party members. He attempts discovering how to articulate his outrage at economic injustice and what his specific function in the struggle for rebellion should be. George's problem as a Communist is not to learn the face of the enemy, but to understand the nature of the working man, and of others connected with the movement. One source of the confusion he feels through most of the book is his lack of insight into those he thinks should be and are his radical allies. Through painful trial and error he learns not to trust either the "professional agitators, the poetic epicureans and parlor orators," nor wholeheartedly as a group the laboring masses. The first are too far from economic pain; the second, too close. One feels no violent need to fight for survival; the other is too tired from the struggle to survive to accept or to understand the necessary strategy of rebellion.

The society of middle-class esthetes and intellectual radicals is represented by Ann Rubens and Myron Cohen. Ann is George's lover; Myron, a radical magazine editor. Both characters also represent tendencies in George and, one suspects, in Bodenheim himself. Ann is art and non-involvement; Myron is cool, theoretic, intellectual involvement. Ann is a devil's advocate. George admits that her attacks on his ideas turn him into a soapbox orator. "You fling your words at me and I call them fastidious sophistries but sometimes I can't answer them," he tells her.

Each challenges the other's generalities. George condemns Ann's lack of concern: "Christ, you make me sick. Millions of people are breaking their spines in a million, stinking factories. Millions of people are sweating and rotting . . . together all over the world, and you . . . you sit here, twirling your sweet little epigrams. . . . Why don't you throw your poems into the nearest ash-can and fight for human beings? Millions of human beings, killing one another in the trenches because they've been doped with lies and hatred. Millions of them, working their chests out to keep the wise ones fat."

But Ann pricks the bubble of George's human reckoning: " 'Honest,' she says, 'you remind me of a social banker, George. You're always talking in millions. It's funny. Those masses are joined in a kind of mystic unit to you, but it isn't true. Nothing except their fears has any power to bring them together. They were killing and robbing each other five thousand years ago and they haven't changed their habits one single inch.' " Bodenheim creates no straw antagonist in Ann. Though George is the book's ultimate hero and Ann finally a kind of turncoat, the dialogues between the two end in a standoff. George grows in knowledge when he admits that Ann is partly right, but that her truth is limited. George's communism finally transcends many of Ann's arguments but never really destroys them.

Myron Cohen is far more involved than Ann, but he constantly tries justifying his position as an editor-leader above the battleground of class warfare. He huffs that, if he could aid the cause better by getting out of his editor's chair and really fighting, he would do so. But, while "he had a prodigious and fiercely sentimental sympathy for men and women who toiled with their arms and legs," his own life "had held little of manual labor, of the wrenched-out gasp that comes when the whistle blows." He affects workingmen's clothes to identify with the laboring classes, but he rents a "re-modeled rooming-house with a studio front and artificial shrubs at the entrance." But Cohen is not essentially a poseur. Even with financial success after writing a bestseller, he devotes nearly all his energies to communism, and his radical spirit is still uncorrupted. He sticks to his journalist's tasks and avoids "the haunts where successful writers and pundits clinked tea-cups and cocktail glasses to banish the shadowy sense of deceit and prostration."

George is clearly Communistic, believing in class warfare and in the inevitable, classless society. "Perhaps I'll live to be eighty," he says, "and still see the same capitalistic bone-grinder all over the world, but there'll be a new gang and a new fight no matter what happens. The struggle won't end until the earth's a peaceful place owned by all the people on it." Yet he is no "mockup" of a model Communist. Part of his antagonism to Ann is that she is socially blind: part is also that she is artistically successful. His own social energies are intensified by his failure as an artist. Perhaps here he reflects Bodenheim. George tells Ann after one of their arguments, "I wish I could give you my sympathy and my hatred, and take your ability in return." He sees brutality among the oppressors of the Communist party, but also weakness among the members. After a policeman clubs and arrests George for demonstrating, he is tried along with fellow agitators. Later he remembers the "judge, who had handled each case as though he were squashing insects which had dared to crawl into the . . . purity of his vision": but he also remembers "the weaponless confusion and oscillation among his fellow communists."

Stages in George's progress as a Communist are depicted in his attitudes toward Ann. He temporarily rejects Ann when he travels south. He leaves the South to help the party but also because he has been defeated locally and wants to return to his old love. When he returns to New York, he goes immediately to Ann's apartment to confront her for the last time. By chance, he meets Ann and her new husband in the street. George still wears his worker's clothes, and Ann's husband, a "cultured materialist," wears a tuxedo. A ripple of reinterest awakens in Ann, and she asks George to call her. She is now at an "Eldorado" number. But George finally rejects her: he does not call. Their love was only a "myth," their love a "chimerical riot." He decides to return to Hurley Heights and to bring back to New York his un-class-conscious yet vaguely rebellious proletariat lover, Kathleen. He will "make her an active rebel and live obscurely beside her for a time, working with her to earn his daily bread with the strength of his arms and legs." The revolution will spring from people like Kathleen, who combines earthy sexual appeal with rough proletarian power.

George learns more than how to combine the sex drive with radicalism as he is educated throughout the book. He learns much about the people he will have to some day organize: "He could understand better now why the revolt was so alien and dim to the lowest masses. The grim job of keeping alive drained their energy. The diggings of physical habit made deeper and deeper grooves from which thought could not rise." He also observes that the cruelty practiced by these masses is only superficial, that the people are often "selfishly kind to one another," that "crisis could wring sacrificial flights from many of them," that they are relatively direct and unspoiled. George also sees their crude jingoism, their racial bigotry, their tindery readiness to ignite into a mob "where each woman and man lost the sore smallness—lost it in the unit of one self-avenging claw." George finally learns that, while conditions may demand violent overthrow, the people are clearly not ready for such rebellion.

Yet while George is outraged at economic injustice and believes firmly in its inevitable decline, he operates strictly on his own, and he appears completely ignorant of party purposes and discipline. He has no faith in the working class's ability to reason out political matters—or anything else. With rare exceptions, he inspires nothing but antagonism in the workers he meets; and he feels that in no way can he overcome this hatred. Yet he knows that eventually, in some distant future, the capitalistic system will crumble and somehow the workers will realize the necessity of banding together. He does not want to submit as a non-worker to outside Communist authority and is in large degree unaware of the nature of that authority. Bodenheim shared this inability to accept authority. As narrator, he criticizes Myron Cohen for operating on the basis that "anything short of complete control within his faction was unthinkable."

The book's imagery underscores the reasons for George's radical view of American life and indicates the necessity for his Com-

munist (or Communist *manqué*) vision, emphasizing the grinding
deadness of worker's life under the capitalistic industrial system
and the artificiality and luxury in the middle-class world. The
Southern mill where George works is described in waste-land
terms: "The bricks, once red, had been browned to a shade of
soulless patience. Hillocks of cinders and ashes reposed in one
corner of the board-fenced enclosure." The workers fight themselves and not their superiors; and, once the work-whistle blows,
the laborer finds himself "a browbeaten human cog, robbed of his
big words and blares, and revolving obediently in the grinding-
process." Most of the workers are defeated or crushed by the
grinding. One woman, trying to celebrate her first birthday party
in ten years, smiles "a rubbery smile with no happiness in it . . .
practicing hilarities without feeling them." Her husband sits in a
wheel chair, rendered literally impotent by the factory system,
paralyzed from the waist down. A very few workers wait quietly
for the chance to regain their rights as human beings. These few
George can reach.

A dominant image describing urban-capitalistic New York depicts a cold and brutal place dwarfing the individual, and a pretentious façade that tries to shield from the outsiders the corruption within. This apartment-house civilization even has an old,
expensively dressed soldier to guard it. George stops in his hobo
clothes in front of such a "towering apartment-hotel, with a green
canopy extending from the entrance to the curb and a rubber mat
underneath the canopy." The apartment dwellers are thus insulated from the real world, from earth or sky. "The marble-square
entrance [was] flanked by artificial shrubs in stone urns. . . . The
elderly doorman in pale blue cloth and silver braid offended him
and yet was humorous, like a tin soldier."

Like most radical novels of the 1930's, *Run, Sheep, Run* contains one crucial scene of social warfare presenting the natural
outcome of tyranically oppressive conditions and foreshadowing
the Marxist apocalypse to come. Bodenheim's mob scene divides
the New York section of the book from the Southern mill-town
section. Thus it is structurally central to the book, and also pivotal
in George's life. Bodenheim plunges the reader directly into the
middle of the fighting and never explains the specific cause of
the bloody outburst. The reader's confusion and disorientation

reflect the fighting itself: here are all the tensions finally sprung, here is society going haywire, and for no single known reason. Single battles erupt, flare violently, disappear, and are replaced by other single battles. Neither police nor demonstrators generate a cohesive power.

But Bodenheim clearly directs the reader's sympathies in the individual battles to the underdog citizenry. Brutal police debate only by club, and strike indiscriminately: "The first policeman twisted his fingers into hair on her head, forcing her to rise again. Each man caught one of her arms and dragged her along. She swung her heel down on the first man's instep. His club cracked against one of her knees. She sagged forward, unconscious now." Some police realize the inhumanity of their actions, but continue to beat down the demonstration: "A mammoth detective listened with a sneer on his pick-axe face. His eyes were ashamed." But the club descends anyway, again and again. At least once it hits a completely innocent bystander, who probably represents the middle-class, white-collar worker also crushed by the system he thinks he helps run.

The police are effective in quelling the immediate and highly disorganized riot, yet actually they only defeat themselves. George emerges from the fight with a clearer notion of what he must do. The innocent, clubbed man will understand the system better for having seen its naked power in action. Others also have their reactions against the system crystallized. One young agitator at first runs "aimlessly in circles, innocently aping a hysteria which he did not feel." He carries a sign saying "Boys and Girls of New York, join the Young Pioneers. The Boy Scouts and Campfire Girls Want to Train you to Become Nurses and Gun-Fodder." He too is beaten, and this beating will be the start of his radical education.

The riot ends slowly. While the chaos is plunged into as the middle of some epic rout, Bodenheim carefully dissolves out of the action. From a noisy crescendo of screaming and skull-cracking, the riot becomes more and more sporadic. A few agitators are caught, but most scamper or scuttle singly away. The city exists as it had before. The aftermath of temporary failure finds no defeated littered about. This rehearsal for rebellion shows disorganization, a lack of numbers and weapons, and a vicious, relentless enemy. But clearly, the guerrilla warfare will continue.

Bodenheim does not present a full-scale analysis of America's economic and social ills in *Run, Sheep, Run*. He does not present the standard radical view toward the classes. Ann, for example, is middle class and antagonistic to communism; but she becomes involved in the riot on George's side. The working class is itself less sensitive to understanding the key to its predicament than are the New York intellectuals who avoid Communist causes. The book contains no hint of a strike; instead, society runs blindly amuck, as in Nathanael West's *The Day of the Locust* (1939). What Bodenheim presents is an individual pitting his mind and body against the system. He portrays not an ideal radical but a young man who might be of use some day, who presently works contrary to the discipline necessary to any group movement, who at the book's conclusion has a strong sense of the realities of the working class's predicament.

Run, Sheep, Run contains swatches of bad writing, as do all Bodenheim's books. When in passion's heat George and Ann kiss each other's knees with great ardor, the language is silly. Despite the occasionally clumsy picture of sex, the over-all honesty of Bodenheim's presentation is impressive. The structure, imagery, and characterization are all controlled. In displaying Communist party squabbles, intellectual sniping, the oppression of mill hands, and especially in following George's career as a radical learning from those around him but working pretty much on his own, Bodenheim succeeds in constructing an unspectacular but vigorous and honest radical novel.

III New York Madness *(1933)*

While *Run, Sheep, Run* is a serious attempt to portray the Depression conditions, *New York Madness* (1933) is not. The book is filled with violence and sensationalism, but both seem calculated, and inapposite to a historic evaluation of the contemporary conditions. The book is curiously old-fashioned in tone, revealing little true social consciousness or political awareness. Although several passing references are made to the Depression, the major characters are well-fed and economically content. In portraying Alicia McCulley's quest for satisfaction—an almost purely sexual search—Bodenheim travels around New York City and Greenwich Village, occasionally presenting a fight or a seduction, taking time out to attack his critics, and etching sometimes amusing, sometimes compulsively insulting pictures of fellow New Yorkers. His sentences are occasionally incoherent: "Alicia McCulley was bored, mournful, even gangrenous, but in every accidental collision between conditions, each one became less convinced of its reality and strove to strengthen itself in the confusion of mutual insult." The characters and situations are too clearly worked from earlier material: Alicia has the intellect and yearnings of Blanche Palmer with the sexual precosity of Jessica Maringold. The man she ultimately finds happiness with is a sensitive cripple, as was Ernest Maller in *Replenishing Jessica.*

The language of *New York Madness* falls back on pseudo-tough dialogue with stilted transitions: " 'Did you pay anything to this jane?' The accomplice simulated a modicum of reluctant oppression. 'Come on, spit it out before I take a sock at you. . . . Talk up, or I'll bust your nose in for you.' " The city is described in familiarly ugly imagery: a building is like "an impressively petrified arm" or "an uplifted, gray talon." One character has "a protective hardness, forced upon her by the neurosis of a sordid city"; but the city is not so much a force as a backdrop for sensational puppets. The most significant sentence of the book occurs when a minor character says that only four classes of women exist: "the housewife, the prostitute, the partly sterilized intellectual, and the turbulent vagabond." The categories note the major female types found throughout Bodenheim's fiction, but one sentence cannot justify a book.

IV   Slow Vision (*1934*)

Bodenheim's last novel, *Slow Vision,* resembles *Georgie May* in its powerful delineation of individual and social decay, and *Run, Sheep, Run* in its vigorously anti-capitalistic stance. *Slow Vision* also shows more than any of Bodenheim's other works the terrible strain under which he was working. The book reeks of disillusionment and failure, and it depicts a hopeless parade of numbed Depression derelicts. Though written from a generally radical point of view, the book offers no true way out of the economic chamber

of horrors shown. *Slow Vision* represents a blind corner in Bodenheim's career that he never worked himself out of; for he never
again published fiction.

Bodenheim focuses on two generally unemployed white-collar
workers, Ray Bailey, college-educated and Nordic, and Allene
Baum, a New York Jew. The two love each other, but their love
is constantly thwarted or brutalized by Depression forces. They
exist in a bleak America gone haywire and among baffled workers
who know that something is wrong but not what to do about it.
Like a Greek chorus, the idea that "something was wrong somewhere" reverberates throughout the book. Once the words are
thought by an insane-asylum nurse on erotic prowl as she wonders about the "railroaded" sane inmates daily cracked with wet
towels and strait-jacketed in her asylum with no hope of release:
a perfect image of Bodenheim's Depression America. Ray himself
thinks "something must be wrong when a fellow can't get a
decent wage, can't tell when he's going to be fired, can't look
forward to any promise of happiness. Something is rotten somewhere." A girl waiting to be picked up says hopefully, "Oh, things
will improve, I guess. They've got to," but Bodenheim adds: "her
voice was stagey and impatient."

The predicament's cause is clear: people are "caught within an
economic system, which enslaved and stripped them under pipe-
dreams of freedom and the old bait of civic pride, patriotic fervor." But what to do about the cause must be learned. Ray Bailey
must first become educated in the economics of despair. According to Bodenheim, he must learn that capitalistic patriotism is a
vicious sham. In the meantime, Ray observes the panicky dis-
possessed who try hard to maintain an identity when economically and politically they have none: "Factory girls, shop-girls on
clattering heels, were kidding frantically to distract the slump of
their bodies and the restricted freedom represented by the few
bills, or coins, tucked within their flashy, shoddy pocketbooks." In
another image Bodenheim represents the masses' fears in a des-
iccated society dominated by blind, corrupt forces. Frightened
workers and alcoholic beggars mill in the streets and in the park
where "dry leaves scraped over the walks, and tapped against the
erect statue of Chester Allan Arthur, twenty-first President, in
frock coat, stock, and high collar . . . blackish green with . . .

corrodings—an osbcure, weirdly pompous figure in the history of past thefts, hidden bargainings accepted as national service and statesmanship."

The corruption blights all social and all age levels. Children not innately vicious are infected by "the ever-denying snobbery and material deceit of their environment." An adolescent girl does nothing but "giggle, sniffle, and jabber about nothing in particular for hours unbrokenly, because her environment, with all of its slyly draped, sexual goads and fears, had never shown her any other outlet." The story of youth is a "tragedy of boys and girls betrayed by the swarm of lies . . . and delusions, foisted upon them by an economic system." These emotionally stunted children will eventually become the fat, slack, gray-skinned waitresses and the skinny, narrow-chested tray-carriers with which the novel is peopled. These are not the hope of the future: "A hell of a child-bearer she'd make, after three or four years of this work."

The adults themselves are embittered, often socially rejected or displaced. Allene Baum's father is a good example of the displaced male. He is too kind and too weak to succeed in a materialistic, competitive society, and he has been pushed aside by his wife, who rules the family: "He could no longer remain a boss because, in his world, the male parent was no longer respected after he had proven himself a failure as a provider, money-getter." Morris Baum's failure sours his wife, who as tenement owner dominates whomever she can. Bearing obvious similarity to Bodenheim's father, Morris is the nice guy who loses to aggressive capitalism and a strong woman. He is a *schlemiel* who lacks status as worker or parent. He is by no means the only economic castoff in *Slow Vision*. Characters constantly lose jobs or work as downtrodden lackeys, fill their lives with pipe dreams, or give up completely. One of Allene's friends becomes a prostitute. A moneyless physical wreck, the girl follows a familiar pattern in radical novels where prostitution is both a capitalistic vice in itself and a symbol of the worker's predicament. "It happened thousands of times, every night, in New York alone, in Boston, Chicago, everywhere."

Hopelessness, brute exhaustion, absolute defeat pervade the incidental actions of *Slow Vision*. Simple details of life become travesties played by whipped animals: restaurant "eaters . . . eyed their neighbors . . . with disfavor . . . covert wariness." Fellow workers are "too tired to be really gay." A man swaggers and brags for his "pick-up," but his "compulsion of hope" only "strives to evade the fact that there was no specific basis for it." Everyone seeks and lacks "money, money, money—the great, sickening tom-tom, flesh pulverizer, the grinning siren always chased by millions of calloused hands with broken, dirty fingernails." Few succeed. "They're the slick babies," a wise punk says: "the ones who pay the other fellow to run the risks, and then rake in most of it themselves."

Ray and Allene are not "slick." Bodenheim focuses on their romance to show what the system does to good, intelligent people who are willing to work hard, but who never really get the opportunity because of the breakdown democratic capitalism has inevitably suffered. They try to achieve a normal, happy relationship, but first one is out of work and weak with hunger, and then the other. They travel from New York to Boston to find some kind of employment, but only worsen their condition. Like nearly all the characters in *Slow Vision*, they are "confronted by a sordidness which they had not made themselves, and [were] uncertain concerning who was responsible for its extension on all sides." Theirs is a sad affair, for even in companionship and sex they find the crippling bleakness of their existence. They quarrel constantly and learn that sex is almost destroyed by their plight. "Christ," Ray says, "everything's hard when people haven't any money, and they're all set for loving but they get ill-tempered over every little thing because they're tired out and their nerves are all chopped to pieces

Later they live together unmarried, and conditions are worse. Ray is completely spent from his tedious job as elevator operator; Allene has been walking Boston's cold and snowy streets looking for a job. They bicker all evening and then make up and wonder what is going to happen to them. In bed "they kissed one another, trailed hands over cheek and throat, came closer in the scarcely conscious linking of arms. He wanted to make love to her but a thick, warm, gray blanket was being wrapped and knotted around him slowly, enticing him against the opposite desire, while she, more awake but with her senses also drooping, felt a disappointment too indistinct to be painful and yet . . . it was hellish . . .

[152]

when you were both so tired . . . so, so tired . . . you couldn't even take. . . . They fell back and slept" (ellipsis Bodenheim's).

Bodenheim also focuses on Ray's growing involvement with communism. Ray is at first antagonistic, and one of his primary objections is the party's foreign domination: "I don't believe in what those dirty Reds say—they're only out to smash up the country and let a few, long-whiskered Russians move in and take over the government." He argues against joining a Communist-inspired strike since "it was difficult for him to string along with leaders, most of them foreign born . . . whose real aim was to disrupt the country and win it over to the command of the Russians." But his drift toward communism increases as the Depression deepens and as he sees that the politics of capitalism offer no way out. For a time he hopes that "maybe a third Party at the next election, headed by Roosevelt himself" can bring improvement, but this hope is never more than a tenuous wish. One of the book's chief villains is, in fact, Roosevelt's National Recovery Act. One girl who works in an N.R.A. lunchroom receives, according to the code, a two-dollar raise. The management then deducts fifty cents for cleaning her aprons and stretches her eight-hour workday to nine or ten hours. Workers who complain receive the runaround from N.R.A. officials while "well-clad, uppish-faced" management men are given quick help.

Ray's eventual initiation into communism is hastened by his realization that those who dissent mildly, in ways recognized by capitalistic society, are ineffectual. Again and again Ray learns that unions are as corrupt as the society that permits them. He hears a worker call for "an honest-to-God union, too, and not a union with a bunch of labor-pimps taking in our dues and living on the fat, and then telling us not to go on strike until they talk it over with the bosses." Socialist leaders also comply in the general betrayal of the worker; their demagogues preach peace and patience and gloat over improvements wrought by the N.R.A.

One by one the props of capitalistic democracy are revealed as decadent to Ray. His conversion to communism begins when he realizes that there is for him no alternative way to beat the system. Even then he does not declare directly for communism; he decides to support a strike called by Communists, and he takes his radical stand in a speech that concludes his part in the novel.

Where Allene asks if he hasn't gone over to the Reds, he answers:

> I haven't made up my mind about that, but I'm going to tell you one thing—this goddam flagwaving is beginning to get under my skin. They pull it every time they're looking for an excuse to hold a worker down. . . . about the only time they ever pay any real attention to a worker is when they're asking him to pick up a gun and go get killed in a war. I don't know whether Communism's the solution or not, but believe me I'm going to read up on it and find out what it's all about before I'm through.

Allene answers: "Well, God knows its not going to hurt either of us if we do, because we know perfectly well that everything else is rotten." Their conversion is almost certain.

Slow Vision was Bodenheim's last published novel, and one of his most powerful. His unremitting and relentless pursuit of Depression neurasthenia effectively reproduces one aspect of the times. With a relative absence of authorial intrusion, he portrays the bewilderment of the most prosperous nation in the world. After a few false starts where he follows minor characters of no significance, he projects in a technically straightforward manner a harsh, grainy newsreel of psychological, familial, and communal breakdown. He makes, as always, some mistakes in diction; and once he starts a scene describing a family of three children but ends with only two. Yet in an almost plodding way he presents life in the lower depths as he thought he saw it lived in those years. He recaptures the baffled insecurity so many felt throughout the dazed, bewildered country.

Bodenheim's fidelity to his personal vision perhaps precluded general success for the book despite its virtues. Since Communist policy shifted so often during the 1930's—and also shortly after the book's publication—the work could not for long embody the Communist party view. Some opinions, such as Bodenheim's relatively gentle view of Roosevelt, in the book were not official policy even at the time of publication. The one party member described in the text is far from an ideal. So the work could never be wholeheartedly embraced as a Communistic document.

Compared to such a book as Steinbeck's *Grapes of Wrath*, *Slow Vision* lacks liberal uplift and the dignity of characterization so necessary to popularly acceptable Depression fiction. *Slow Vision*

is a cold, pitiless book that affirms no noble concept of man. Bodenheim's leading characters are not completely defeated, but
they are thoroughly whipped for the time. They continue more
out of desperation than hope. Even a brief note of optimism at the
conclusion of the novel is muted to become ultimately part of
the wretched existence of Allene and Ray. After Ray reveals his
radical plans and Allene agrees that things could not be worse,
they look out from their depressing flat into the wintry Boston
street of night and see only despair: "She leaned against his
shoulder and they stared through the window at the drizzle of
rain outside, the stooping, tight-faced figures hurrying down the
street." Thus the book offers no cathartic action or bright hope,
only Depression stupor and the faintest glimmer of a better
future. That glimmer would burst into light for the country, but
not for Bodenheim.

CHAPTER 6

Last Years and Last Poems

THE partial success of Bodenheim's first works in the 1930's was misleading. In the wake of this momentary recognition, Bodenheim drifted through the 1930's for the most part jobless and almost unknown, another dead artifact of the Jazz Age. Life in the Village was no longer fun nor cheap, and he could not support himself, much less a wife and child. Uneducated and unskilled in business, troublesome and generally unprofitable to publishers—that scheme to please typists and factory girls, if it existed, clearly was ineffective—and temperamentally unsuited to regular employment, he somehow existed.

A letter to his wife, written sometime after he broke with Liveright in 1932, chronicles his broken health and spirit, his pitiful hopes to alchemize the Hollywood rainbow. From Los Angeles he wrote:

Arrived here, sick and coughing. . . . My future is hazy. I've discovered that I have bronchitis, and I must not go about much for the next week or two. A man connected in a minor way with a Hollywood firm is taking my novels to a prominent, influential agent here. The man will pose to the agent as my secretary, with the story that I am simply here on a sojourn to recover my health. Everything must be done with an elaborate indirectness, and the author cannot even besiege the agent's offices, lest he convey an impression of over-eager inferiority. Anyway, I will be in the background, temporarily, and my novels will be in the hands of people who know the movie-ropes thoroughly. The rest will be a matter of whether the movie companies believe that my reputation and work contain an audience appeal, or not. . . . I'm doing nothing but resting and awaiting developments, as I'm very sick, and nervously broken down. I'll mend rapidly, though. I send you my love, dear. If I write only once a week, understand and don't worry.

Not long after he reported more of the feeble farce: "The Fox concern has turned down all of the novels and they are now scattered with other companies. Metro-Goldwyn is still seriously considering *Replenishing Jessica,* but a man named Thalberg [Irving Thalberg, production head of the company] has the final say there, and he has told my agents that he will give them a final decision next week (he seems to be wavering). My position has become untenable here. The people with whom I'm staying can scarcely scrape their bread together, and I can't impose on them much longer." Thalberg—if he ever saw the novel—declined; and Bodenheim left Los Angeles with its rainbow still a vapor leading to no gold. The next year he briefly returned and placed a wreath on Fedya Ramsay's grave in Santa Barbara. His most positive accomplishment in California was to commemorate a woman dead twenty years.

Back in New York, he read poems for food at Max Gordon's Village Vanguard which had just opened in February, 1934, at 1 Charles Street. His old friends John Rose Gildea, vagabond Harry Kemp, and other indigent poets also read there. Bodenheim was the star attraction, in a red tie and blue shirt, at Francis McCrudden's Raven Poetry Circle through the 1930's. Along with Gildea, Jane O'Ryan, Anton Romatka, and others, he tacked his poems on a fence at Thompson Street and Washington Square South. MacKinlay Kantor remembers seeing Bodenheim around the mid-1930's at the Poetry Circle, sprawling dull-eyed, with swollen ankles. Above him five or six poems were stuck, and over and over Bodenheim muttered "poems by Maxwell Bodenheim twenty-five cents, poems by Maxwell Bodenheim twenty-five cents. Autograph copy fifty cents, autograph copy fifty cents."

In 1935 Bodenheim received some publicity by complaining to city officials of the inadequacy of his relief allowance—fourteen dollars a month for lodging and five dollars every other week for food. Later the same year he commanded a small bobtail army of writers who assaulted City Hall about the same problem. The New York press elected him "mayor" of New York City—the poet was a joke—and some plans were talked about to send the sick writer West, but no temporary relief could halt his descent, and the plan sputtered out anyway.

Still he wrote poetry. The Oscar Blumenthal Award, given by

Poetry Magazine in 1939 "for a poem or group of poems published" in the magazine, must have pleased him—Dylan Thomas had won the year before—and the award was no gesture. The one hundred dollars kept him in food and liquor for a while. So once again he had serious recognition; and, after being divorced by Minna in 1938 and marrying, in 1939, family responsibilities. Even after Bodenheim clearly was incapable of any kind of decent, stable home relationship, he had corresponded with Minna. He was throughout his life emotionally tied to her, as she was in some ways to him. But their life together was impossible, and she must have seen that, like most self-destructive people, he would only destroy her in time, so that their painful break was inevitable. Solbert knew his father's disgraces better than his love, and their break was more complete.

Bodenheim loved them both: his life and letters demonstrate his devotion, but he was incapable of manifesting his love in any consistent, balanced way. Years after the break, when Minna still saw her former husband on the street occasionally (his second wife forbade any other kind of meeing, and Bodenheim sadly obeyed), Bodenheim mentioned that he had always helped when he could; he had done what was for him possible. But, when Minna told him the truth—that he was never there when needed—Bodenheim looked at her as blankly as a foreigner who did not understand her language.

When he married Grace Fawcett Finan, he married a diabetic with a small income whose need for him proved great. Midway through their marriage, Grace was discovered to be cancerous; and Bodenheim, when he was able, nursed her tenderly during her illness. She also provided one of his many excuses for living— a paradox of his life was the tenacity with which he clung to existence while punishing himself to the point of destruction. To Ben Hecht, as reported in *Child of the Century*, Bodenheim confided that he would commit suicide were it not that his wife needed him.

Shortly after Bodenheim married Mrs. Finan, whose artist-husband had worked with him on a Federal Writers' Project in New York City, he was fired from the Bibliographies and Indices Project for having fraudulently signed an affidavit that he was not a Communist. Bodenheim claimed that whatever ties he had to the party had been broken. When he said this, in August, 1940, he undoubtedly told the truth. Throughout the 1930's he was not classed as a radical and rarely if ever took part in the various movements and internecine wars common to radically involved writers that Aaron and Rideout have ably chronicled.[1] Bodenheim was not even among the writers and intellectuals who signed the telegram to Coolidge in 1927 asking a stay of the execution of Sacco and Vanzetti.

Bodenheim published in liberal-radical magazines such as the *Liberator*, but his work was differentiated by editor Joseph Freeman from that of the true radicals like Floyd Dell and Mike Gold. To Freeman, Bodenheim was simply a literary experimenter. Into the 1930's he shifted from what had been an anti-Communist position to being a fellow traveler, attracted as were so many intellectuals to communism's radical cures for the deep and obvious ills of capitalist America. For a writer, for such an economic underdog as he had become, avoiding some shade of Red would have been difficult in those terrible times. As Frederick Hoffman says in *The Twenties*, "even Maxwell Bodenheim marched in proletarian parades up Fifth Avenue in the Thirties." Joseph Freeman could only conjecture, in an unpublished letter, whether Bodenheim carried a card. In the anthology *Proletarian Literature*, edited by Granville Hicks, Bodenheim's "To a Revolutionary Girl" was reprinted; and Bodenheim was referred to as "the author of a number of novels, including *Slow Vision*," his most radical work.

Undoubtedly communism offered him some handy surface reasons for his failure as writer and person. Whatever connection he may have had was emotional, not cerebral. His individualism was too strong, even decayed as he was, to submerge itself completely in any mass ideology. His poems and stories show radical tendencies from about 1932, but they are in no ways documents of American Marxism. His attraction was never wholehearted. And, as Floyd Dell has written recently in a letter, "maybe he thought things too bad to be cured"; a feeling absolutely inconsistent with Marxism. With no formal education, unloved as a child, surrounded and ground down by poverty, rebellious, anti-authoritarian, in his own eyes a failure, Bodenheim was ripe for communism. But his commitment was strangely shaky and sporadic at best.

After a brief, happy period in Brooklyn with Grace, Bodenheim snuffled and croaked his way through the 1940's, drunkenly lamenting his spiritual and physical sickness: "I have a malady of the soul," he muttered; "I have a scarecrow body and a dead soul." He sold poems for drinks at the San Remo or Minetta Tavern, since whiskey is cheaper and more anodynic than food and, after a while, more of a necessity. Occasionally, he flashed out with a colorful image—he coined the phrase "Greenwich Village is the Coney Island of the soul." He resumed his less-than-amazing acting career in a play written, directed, and produced by William Saroyan at the William Saroyan (originally Belasco) Theater, as part of the Saroyan Drama Festival. Playing "A Poet" and reciting an original poem, "Jazz Music," Bodenheim's stage comeback lasted less than a week. *Across the Board on Tomorrow Morning* had almost a longer title than run. It opened August 17, 1942, and closed August 22. Canada Lee's performance was praised; Bodenheim's was not.

With his wife's aid, he managed to have *Lights in the Valley* published also in 1942, but most critics ignored the book. The *Poetry* reviewer allowed Bodenheim his vaguely radical ideology, but argued that "in most other technical respects—metrically, for example—he is, by my reading, dull, imitative, and obvious."[2] Though the book's obviousness did not prevent the reviewer from misreading several poems, the poetry lacked sparkle. But the reviewer was correct about the poems' technical orthodoxies. As Bodenheim resembled more and more a Zolaesque misfit, bludgeoned by gin and a brutal life, his work became increasingly conventional. His age, and perhaps his latent nationalism, drew him to Harding "normalcy" in other ways.

He wrote, for example, letters to the New York *Daily News* "Voice of the People" column expressing a kind of "B" movie patriotism. On January 17, 1945, a letter captioned "Max on War Aims" bristled with jingoism: "You are anxious to know what we are fighting for. We are fighting to tame and cage jungle animal Japs and Nazis who murder our surrendered soldiers, bomb our military hospitals, starve and torture American children and shoot them down, and violate every known rule of ethics and civilization. Until these animals are completely defeated, the threat of a return to barbarism will continue to hover over us."

Dissipated as he was, Bodenheim continued to write and revise his poetry. In 1944, Thomas Yoseloff published him as one of *Seven Poets in Search of an Answer*, a People's Front anthology when such thinking was patriotic. Among the other poets were Bodenheim's old friend Alfred Kreymborg, Langston Hughes, and Aaron Kramer. Poems not by Bodenheim included "Good Morning, Stalingrad," "Guernica," "Song for Federico García Lorca," and "The International Brigade."[3] In 1946, the *Selected Poems* were published, for which he revised many of his earlier poems. A kind of official, historic recognition was also his when on June 1, 1945, he recorded several of his poems in Studio A of the Library of Congress.

I *"Last Poems"*

Lights in the Valley and Bodenheim's portion of *Seven Poets in Search of an Answer* are combined in the *Selected Poems* as "Poems of Social Message," and must be treated together as such. His work is generally competent, and less rhetorically flamboyant than his earlier poems. Gone are the flashy metaphors driven together by sheer poetic verve. Instead, the poetry shows the desire to communicate social messages to other artists and men. Bodenheim seems compelled to employ rhythms and rhymes that do not call attention to themselves. He even avoids free verse: poem after poem uses iambics, with *abab* exact rhyme.

Three concerns dominate his work: criticism of his generation of artists and of himself for lacking social consciousness; direct social criticism of the American scene; and attacks on war. His point of view is not formally Communistic, and no coherent social theory emerges from the various poems. They are, instead, the work of a man who is sometimes emotionally attracted to the movement, who thinks he sees a society gone mad, who sees himself alone and a failure, who knows something, everything, is wrong and wants to attack. But the poems have only the most general relevance to the basic tenets of communism. They reveal little militancy, no suggestion of American class warfare, no investigation of economic forces invariably in dialectic confrontation. Even at the height of the Popular Front movement his social message is that war is evil, that inequality is unjust, and that artists cannot afford to remain aloof in a world out of whack, but that they must concern themselves with the social obligations of art.

The last theme he returns to again and again. In "One Generation," for example, he forcefully characterizes those writers of his time who earlier had "strolled in mysticism's Sunday best,/ Threadbare beneath, but subtle, radiant, lean." They fought their small battles but not the central, crucial ones: "We swept Main Street of shams and bric-a-bracs/ And slew vulgarities—tin sword crusades." In their war, success was always qualified, compromised; for they capitulated for limited victory and petty artistic triumph. "We were not happy, peace was never gained/ Without surrender—flimsy, gorgeous fare—/ And when the crumbs were scattered and it rained,/ We sat with sophistries, played solitaire."

Throughout his career Bodenheim was a vocal anti-intellectual. In "Poems of Social Message" he attacks intellectuals for not mingling with the masses with whom they have lost contact, for not being friends to man, for "never join[ing] the bleachers at a game,/ Coatless, perspiring. . . . Sharing a rich excitement." Joining the masses was something the early Bodenheim himself would never have done, certainly in his poetry. In the same poem, "Friendly Message to Intellectuals," he also reverses himself in stating that "life remains long after art-works die,/ And their creators are no longer names/ Because they fashioned Truth from walls too high," apparently beyond reach of the people. From this new vantage-point of social consciousness, even the poet's view of nature changes. No longer is nature important for itself or for the personal emotions it inspires. In "Different Ivory-Tower" Bodenheim states the new awareness that "only dwarfs, and children dream alone/ On hemstiched hills, laced dells, year after year/ When tigers plague the world and people moan." The poet must go to nature "Not for the long peace veiling emptiness—/ But for replenishment, the marrying/ Of heart and earth beyond elusive stress." This poetry is Wordsworth-cum-Marx. The poet needs occasional resanctification in nature, to more effectively plunge back into the bitterly struggling society.

But the poet-artist is not to tarry long in nature. Bodenheim emphasizes this message in three acute verse-letters to John Gould Fletcher, Noel Coward, and Maxwell Anderson. In the first and last of these he employs the nature images of mountain and plain or valley to demonstrate that the artist should locate among the people. To Fletcher, he admonishes "The word Eternity should not be carved/ Upon the heights where poets sometimes stand,/ Watching, too carefully, the semi-starved,/ Slow climbing of the mass on upward sand." The sonnet, dedicated to Fletcher "who wrote of 'eternal politics' and the mystic separation of the poet," concludes with the poet's departure from the isolated, uninvolved heights: "When Byron left the beauty of the lark/ To fight in foreign land, he understood/ That poetry will never fly, increase/ Until the bottom source knows lasting peace." The "bottom source" is the people of the plain, perhaps Sandburg's "the people, yes."

"To Maxwell Anderson" also uses the mountain-valley split: "I passed High Tor, half-mountain taking green/ Blunt-shouldered, bending down to question/ The Hudson River" the poem begins, alluding to *High Tor*, the hero of which wants a mountain to house his individuality. Bodenheim admits that the mountain is removed "from cynicism, intrigue, doubting"; and he implies by synecdoche that its inhabitant is too. But he sharply criticizes the brand of idealism such a hero displays: "This brain of ours too often can mistake/ Selfishness for idealism/ Unhurt in loftiness, afraid to make/ The compromise of realism." Therefore, the true artist must be vulnerable, must submit to the dangers of valley life among the people: "Poetry must go back to the night/ Upon the lowlands, unprotected." The poem's message is, of course, open to question. But Bodenheim simply draws forth the mountain-valley image into a coherent, plausible point of view.

Bodenheim recaptures somewhat less fairly but more amusingly the artistic milieu of another contemporary in "Dear Noel Coward." The poem opens with one of the rare puns in Bodenheim's social poetry, on "gay," that carries implications of pleasure achieved through evasion, and suggests the grotesqueness of homosexual irresponsibility: "You know the men, deliberately gay,/ Who sleep within the eager hum of dawn;/ Whose hearts and minds find, prematurely gray,/ The cross between a snicker and a yawn." "Cross" also puns, for the last image can mean that the men find the cross—the combination—of snicker and yawn, of cynical antagonism and total indifference; or it can mean that the men locate the cross of their religion in bored cynicism. Then

Bodenheim less successfully describes the "women playing with remorse,/ The ladies suave and secretly afraid,/ Compared to whom, Godiva on her horse/ Would be a damsel sumptuously arrayed." The "to whom" obtrudes, and the Godiva image is forced, though it does connote sexual looseness that complements the "gay" pun. But immediately Bodenheim's tone becomes unplayful, more direct and almost hortatory, in lines of prophetic and explicit chill: "There is a vengeance destined for those men/ Who flippantly ignore injustice, pain./ The acid into which they dip their pen/ Sinks into age and makes them weak again." Aloof and inactive, they stand, their fate lurking "in that cold hour where decision forms,/ Certain and terrible, beyond escape."[4]

Bodenheim also recognizes his own earlier social unawareness. In "Renunciation," a poem of unusual simplicity and directness, he recants, but with longing, the old poetic stance from which he had viewed the universe and escaped the horrors of life around him. He begins with his life as a child and young poet, and tells how easy it was to lapse from the real world into beautiful make-believe, to live in a tower-room and look up instead of down: "I was a mystic once, the fine/ Star-patterned slantings of a dream/ Dropped to my attic room—design/ To pacify our earthly scheme./ That this huge wistfulness dies slow,/ I know. . . ./ My childhood prayers, cancelling/ First hints of ugliness, became/ The borrowed shrine where thoughts could sing,/ Where lies could vanish, ending shame." But the house he now lives in does not permit such pretty and exalted escape: "Walk into this house, resent/ This scavenging—old hands dump out/ A can of beef stamped government." Outside the house are other miseries to record—a dead Negro woman, a flayed union man.

Then the poet makes what should have been his final point: "What time have we for quarrel, loss,/ When crucifixions multiply/ Beyond the Roman nail and cross." Bodenheim's contrast between the heavily formal and Latinate "crucifixions multiply" and the terse, simple Saxon "nail and cross" is especially effective, emphasizing the brute reality of endless martyrdom. The poem's total effect is somewhat minimized by the final nine lines of now gratuitous, anticlimactic message—"Let us be watchful lest we die/ With eyes glued on the universe." But the work still contains great impact, not because of the possible rightness of the poet's advice, but because of the acuteness of his confession.

"Sonnet" begins by describing the loneliness of such a writer as Bodenheim, or Ben Hecht, had been, who "swung the small, blunt knife of ridicule/ To hide the effervescence of a soul/ Immersed in gaudy tatters." This writer—and now the poem no longer applies to Bodenheim—eventually makes money, producing "Thin novels, brittle swaggering of plays,/ Cartoons of enemies, with malice, stealth. . . . /Yet in this ease he found himself still poor,/ Begging for friendship, shivering, insecure." "Poet's Story," another sonnet, presents a sharper image of Bodenheim than had "Sonnet." He describes his early poetry as that in which "moderate truths and honesties/ Were married, raised their families of verse./ They hated blusterings and diplomacies,/ The bold, smooth pose that brings a bulging purse." But then, in the poet's "middle life," the "Bitter, improvising violin. . . ./ Found steadier consents,/ Not tamed, but gained armor, discipline." Now the new Bodenheim walks proudly in strange and impressive company: "Walt Whitman, Plato, Baudelaire,/ Close, compromising in a forward stare."

The poetry such a sensitive, socially aware poet should write is demonstrated in Bodenheim's anti-Fascist war poems that span early European conflicts, the Spanish Civil War and World War II. He does not in these poems espouse specifically Russian ideology, and he never mentions Communist Russia at all. He does, however, in three sonnets, focus on the peasant class and its ultimate rise. I suspect he found peasant causes more palatable than those of the American lower class. Each of the sonnets centers on violent death occurring in a natural landscape that is intended to display only beauty or fruitfulness. In one, "peach blossoms gleam" on "rotting bodies" in a ditch. "A peasant sprawls, grotesquely torn apart" by a bomb, and the peasant's horse stands by waiting to be hitched to the plow. Spring will eventually return and "clean these wasted lands," and other peasants will return too, "linking hands," standing "clear-eyed" to "chain the old returning over-lords." The anti-war sonnets are often direct and honest, but they lack the intensity the form demands. Bodenheim's images, while not flat or precious, are sometimes too conventional to portray with esthetic effectiveness the immediacy and horror of war. Mere invocation of victorious peasantry is similarly undramatic, and almost a stereotyped cartoon.

"Poem to Gentiles" achieves greater intensity and immediacy, though it is a longer work. In its beginning, especially, it well enlists art to the side of social consciousness. Dealing with two recurrent concepts of Bodenheim's later poetry—the horror of war and the viciousness of racial or religious prejudice—the poem is far more than a rhetorical statement of objections; it is a vigorous presentation of conditions. Bodenheim begins the poem in a quiet and calm tone, as though he were simply commenting on known fact. This technique generates great tension because of the disparity between what his imagery is depicting and the cold tone of statement: "The butchering must be wholesale and the smell/ Of dead Jews strong enough to drift,/ Like vastly stifled echoes of a yell,/ Before the easy, widespread protests lift." The butcher image is, of course, common; but, linked with the calculated politeness of observation, it becomes especially vicious, as though one must be careful to measure the exact moment before the pleasures of bigotry succumb to sickness of the soul. Continuing in a rational manner, Bodenheim divides the future protesters into two classes: the leaders, "mountebanks,/ Smooth men who plot the time to cheer or kneel," who wait "Until the slaughter-house revolves for years/ And business lags because supplies are slow"; and the common masses, "little, harried men, depleted, glued/ By warm and cumbersome monotonies," who, when they finally "shake hands with Jews, the hard worn touch is real." The prophesied handshaking occurs because of shared stress, the common bond of the underdogs. The handshaking occurs in battle, or at home after hearing word of a dead son.

As in his other books, Bodenheim criticizes American life generally in his "Poems of Social Message." Sometimes the criticism is light. "Upper Family" delightfully tells in mostly two-step rhythm the horror of a good uppercrust family at seeing their son turn Socialist. "In Nineteen Hundred they preferred/ Parchesi, lottoes, and charades./ The ladies two-stepped, barely stirred./ The men sneaked down to Bowery shades/ And filled their stovepipe hats with beer." But the son of such a family sees only façade and hypocrisy in these so-called good years. So, as other "sons and daughters tryst," he stepped out and "became a socialist."

"Sincerely Yours, Culture," a collection of five sonnets, offers a bleak panorama of Depression life: a young intellectual on the picket line for the first time finally lunges from his cage of art upon seeing a policeman club his wife; an impoverished musician discovers surprising sympathy in the simple touch of his elderly landlady's hand; a poet destroys his "slim nobilities" to carry his own—and others'—share of "unsolved sufferings." Several poems such as "The Women" or "Technique," are solid, quasi-journalistic accounts of how workers develop a feeling of community that leads them to threaten a strike; how racial prejudice can be manipulated into race riots. Both poems employ a relatively simple narrative style and avoid slogans, though they do not entirely lack the doctrinaire brotherhood of leftist statements.

The sonnet "Spring, 1945" ties up many of Bodenheim's thematic concerns as he describes, with simplicity and accuracy, the aftermath of the war, and tentatively suggests an ultimate peace. The scene he depicts is one of almost unrelieved desolation. Nature as well as man—and the poem's imagery fuses the two—is depleted: "The plows are rusting and the farmers' homes/ Slant, hollow-eyed, in ruins choked by weeds./ Upon the shell-packed fields a lone horse roams,/ Forlornly free yet haunted by old needs." Nature will start again its old cycle, but slowly, meeting death and decay: "The shattered trees wear trails of sickly green/ And, like a hunted child, the scented breath/ Of wild-flowers shrinks within the broken scene/ And, puzzled, meets the ancient stench of death."

But nature can eventually—inevitably must, in fact—swing into its ever-returning pattern. The poem's sestet describes this movement as a march that pauses only momentarily with the harvest, and Bodenheim's iambics similarly march and then stop at harvest: "The seasons march from birth to tranquil crest/ And harvest, and until we emulate/ Their start, their fruitful bloom and snow-capped rest,/ We will be creatures of confusion, hate." Then Bodenheim's concluding couplet states in consciously contorted images man's disharmony, his failure to achieve the ordered ebb and flow of life: "Our own slim, taunted springs grotesquely twined/ With death and wandering, half old and blind."

His sense of history is sharp here. How close the lines would apply to his own bloody harvest he could not know, but his poems throughout his career show that he knew the forces and rhythms of modern life that had sprung others into similarly violent traps.

II *Last Days*

Much of Bodenheim's life throughout the 1940's was spent cadging drinks in the Village. In *Child of the Century*, Ben Hecht described him as "a gaunt, shabby looking man . . . the albino face with the look of frostbite on its skin . . . a jack-o-lantern smile distends his mouth, exposing a number of missing teeth." After his second wife's slow death in 1950, the painters and writers helped him when they could; but he was shattered beyond aid. He somehow lived on into the 1950's, writing mediocre poems and selling them for drinks, his talent lingering just enough to remind him of what he once had. Stringy fleshed and with the glazed eyes of a bum, he was arrested early in 1952 with seven other hobos who were caught sleeping in a subway train. *Time* for February 18 reported this incident under the heading "The Literary Life," and repeated Bodenheim's remarks: "The Village used to have a spirit of Bohemia, gaiety, sadness, beauty, poetry. Now it's just a geographical location." In this location Bodenheim now sometimes walked the streets with an "I am blind" sign.

He still drank at the San Remo and the Minetta Tavern; he wrote poems for tourists, for sight-seeing burghers and coeds down for a jazz weekend. He bickered with friends and other Village oddities such as Professor Seagull (so called because of his impressive bird imitation) Joe Gould.[5] Perhaps the two most notorious "weirdos" in a community of eccentrics, both knew well how to hurt the other. "You're only an artsy-craftsy poet," Gould told him, "a niminy-piminy poet. . . . And you're frightfully un-educated." And Bodenheim said once to Gould, whose lifelong work, the apparently nonexistent *Oral History*, is a mute tribute to his childhood rejection, "Don't tell me you're still trying to bury your father." After the bars closed and the tourists and col-lege students left, Bodenheim might shamble to the Waldorf Cafeteria, on Sixth Avenue near Eighth Street. Here he talked and drank his food—maybe hot water thick with catsup, a kind of spicy tomato soup. Then he would sit like a cadaver under the sickly, yellow-green light that gave the Waldorf its other name, "the waxworks."

In the spring of 1951 another dead soul drifted into the wax-works. Through Ruth Fagan, Bodenheim came ultimately to be cornered by the destruction he had long quested for. Ruth Fagan was about thirty, attractive, and had attended Michigan State College at East Lansing. An exceptionally sympathetic, warm, loving woman, she also had a history of mental disturbance, and had once set fire to her parents' home. Outside the waxworks, the night they met, heavy rain fell; and, as Ruth explained, "he had an umbrella and I did not." She bought a poem from him, and they walked around the Village holding hands. Two days later they announced they were going to be married, and about a week later declared they were man and wife. What queer quirk drove Ruth to marry the sponging, apparently impotent old wreck is not known. Perhaps his decay attracted her; perhaps too, his helplessness and the fact that he had once been someone impor-tant were factors. Max could both love Ruth and be punished by her occasional waywardness. He also saw in her another Minna; for, as Louis Grudin said in a letter, "Even in her mannerisms she resembled Minna, though seemingly without her fiery buoyancy. . . . As Max introduced his new wife he astonished me by asking in gleeful, taunting confidence . . . 'Wouldn't you say she's the image of Minna, eh Lou?' " Grudin also recognized Ruth's in-volvement: "At the second meeting it was she who was the articu-late one, telling me how they had met and making humorous and despairing comments with her eyes and brows as she tossed her head at him, as if to say 'This great bargain of mine, this incorrigi-ble great man, this is what he is, and what am I to do with him?' And she had evidently become as deeply involved as Minna had been; all seemed painfully redundant, foolish, hopeless, and pa-thetically sordid. Max was in a frightening state of tormented physical decay."

In any case, she loved him and tried to help him. They lived for a while at the Colburne Hotel, then were asked to leave. Ruth worked for a time at Brentano's, and sometimes Max worked for Sam Roth, sitting and drinking and ostensibly writing his mem-oirs. They drank together too, and fought; and Ruth too bummed with her husband. They created their own waste land, a world Dorothy Day described in the March, 1954, *Catholic Worker,* of "dirty clothes, rags, dust, cigarette butts . . . onions . . . scuffed shoes, dirty socks." They moved from park benches to rooms on Bleeker Street, kept on drinking, begging, scuffling, and kept on too a perverse and tenderly kind love. Each cheated, Ruth more actively than Max, yet each stuck to the other in inverse symbiosis like coupled leeches. Sporadically, Ruth tried to live in the "upper world," especially at the beginning of their affair. She worked briefly at Macy's, and she invited the poet's mother-in-law to meet her new son. But the eccentricity of Bodenheim's life made ordinary existence impossible, and she seemed incapable of a separate life. So each weighted by the other's live corpse, they plummeted faster.

When Bodenheim was arrested on February 8, 1952, along with the other Skid Row bums, for sleeping in a subway car, Ruth searched the city for his twenty-five-dollar fine. Apparently, she had thrown him out, or he had left her; but they rejoined. In the fall of 1952 they were sent money to attend a reunion celebration of the Chicago Renaissance. Apparently sober and gentle at first, Bodenheim slid quickly into standard behavior. Under the pressure of appearing before old acquaintances and enemies as a normal person, Bodenheim buckled completely; he drank constantly and begged from friends. While he at first read gracious if conventional verses dedicated to his young and equally disheveled wife (by this time the two slept in their clothes), he later bickered with her loudly in public and slapped her face. The writer Vincent Starrett described to Edward DeVoe, Bodenheim's "debauched, alcoholic, and altogether disreputable" appearance: Bodenheim "looked as if he had been buried, or drowned for some weeks: a sort of living dead man." As farce lurched into fiasco, Ruth kept repeatnig "Anyway, I'm Mrs. Maxwell Bodenheim." Finally the unhealthy couple was expelled like a noxious impurity from the collected body of sane authors. If anyone recognized the extent of his physical and moral and psychological deterioration, no one seemed inclined to do anything about him. By then, however, his case was hopeless.

Late in 1952 the Bodenheims left Chicago where forty years before Max had pinned bright promising poems on the *Little Review*'s tent flap. He left with a leg injury just as before he had departed with an arm or shoulderblade break. Years before, Alfred Kreymborg had greeted him and arranged his life; now Ruth attempted desperately to get some money by promoting a reading of Max's poems at the Jabberwocky Cafe on Fourth Street in New York City. A fair crowd gathered, some from respect and some from curiosity to hear the freak. But Bodenheim, either afraid or proud, stumbled from the platform stammering it was too stuffy to read. He had no teeth and not much voice, and few heard his mumbling.

He realized some money trying to write his memoirs for Village publisher Sam Roth, who had gained fame in the 1920's by publishing an unauthorized edition of *Ulysses* for hot-handed esthetes, and who added luster to his reputation by publishing *Jews Must Live*, "an account of the persecution of the world by Israel on all the frontiers of civilization" (one appendix is headed "Do the Jews emit a peculiar odor?" and Roth answers "yes"). Yet Roth helped Bodenheim when few could or would. Bodenheim realized that what memories eked forth were wrung at great expense of his resources, and he could write very little. An old friend who met Bodenheim at this time saw him with the publisher "who had placed a bottle of whisky on the table at Max's elbow, and Max kept pouring and drinking and making frequent hasty trips to the bathroom." The friend and Bodenheim soon left together, to the publisher's disgust. They talked far past midnight, Bodenheim trying to figure some way to extricate himself and retrieve the notes he had managed to write. After Bodenheim's death, a book modestly called *My Life and Loves in Greenwich Village* appeared under Bodenheim's name. The style is clearly unlike anything else he wrote, and the book's editor, Roth (to whom a eulogistic chapter is devoted), suggests in the text that the supposed memoir was prepared from incomplete notes Bodenheim had left. The book should not be considered Bodenheim's.

In February, 1953, as Dorothy Day writes in *Loaves and Fishes*, the Bodenheims sought out Miss Day at the library of her *Catholic Worker;* they had been evicted and needed food and shelter. Probably to ensure receiving aid, Ruth invented the incredible tale that Max had been baptized a Catholic. Receiving asylum from his old friend, the alleged Catholic was baffled at the 12:30 Rosary; he wondered whether the churchgoers "were praying at him, or for him." Miss Day placed the two at Maryfarm, where they stayed about a month until Ruth's sexual enticing of another eager guest became flagrant; and she then moved husband and wife to the Peter Maurin Farm on Staten Island. Bodenheim was an ideal guest, writing sonnets to others at the retreat. Ruth tried selling some of his poems; and once, when the New York *Times* bought one for ten dollars, the entire camp rejoiced. But the pastoral stay could not last indefinitely; and, after Bodenheim's injured leg mended, they left Arcadia for the Village. Shortly after, Ruth returned for their remaining belongings. With her was Harold Weinberg, who would kill both of them.

For a time Bodenheim stumbled corpse-eyed again through his old haunts, shuffling slack-limbed like a caricature from Hogarth's "Gin Lane." He wrote poetry still and sold some for drinks, and he received handouts from old friends such as Louis Cohen, who operated a laundry on West Eleventh Street. Bodenheim always tried to supply poems to repay friends, and Cohen cherished his collection of unpublished Bodenheim manuscripts. Once Bodenheim met Dylan Thomas at the Minetta Tavern, where Oscar Williams had taken the Welsh poet. No spark of recognition snapped between the two who had received the same prize in consecutive years. Bodenheim carried his usual sheaf of poems under an arm bent as though in a sling, clutching under protective wing what was left of his art. He had a bad cold; and, as he read, mucus dripped from his nose, caking like a hideous stalactite. Thomas did what no one else would—he wiped the older poet's nose.

More and more Harold Weinberg was seen with the Bodenheims. At twenty-five, Weinberg had a police record and had been discharged from the army as mentally unfit. He was sexually attracted to Ruth, and Ruth was both attracted to and repelled by Weinberg. During one of the triad's frequent arguments Bodenheim shouted to Weinberg: "leave her alone or I'll kill you." Weinberg rose and said: "you hate me, don't you," and Bodenheim replied, "of course I do." And once, during another fight, Weinberg slashed Bodenheim with a knife. But still they went around together. Bodenheim must have seen the brute horror implicit in the situation, but he did nothing about it.

No one knows completely what happened the night and early morning of February 6 and 7, 1954. What appears to have occurred is that, like a grandiloquent cavalier, Bodenheim made the gratuitous but to him necessary gesture of preserving Ruth's honor. Ruth herself could not fend off the animal she had enticed. No one was sober, and no one was really sane; but Weinberg was fairly strong and used both a gun and a knife. He burst Bodenheim's heart with a twenty-two-rifle bullet that lodged in the dead poet's spine. Ruth clawed and scratched Weinberg, and he stabbed her four times with a long hunting knife. Apparently, no one heard this horror. The double murder was discovered next day by Weinberg's landlord Alfred Luck. Bodenheim had a copy of *The Sea Around Us* on his chest. Weinberg was caught at a friend's house on February 10. Although, after the killings, he had futilely sought to make his crime appear the result of robbery, he proudly raved at the trial that "I ought to get a medal. I killed two Communists." On April 8, Weinberg's brief flight into literary history ended when he was committed to Matteawan State Hospital for the Criminally Insane.

Bodenheim was buried near Oradell, New Jersey, in the Cedar Park Cemetery the same day his killer was caught. Even his death led to bitterness. Ben Hecht announced he was going to pay for the funeral; but, if he did, the records do not show it. Minna Bodenheim paid nearly all the expenses. Alfred Kreymborg, who had been attracted by Bodenheim's youth and spirit four decades past, delivered the eulogy. After comparing Bodenheim to Poe and Heine, he concluded that "he was a great lover and wit. We need not worry about the future. He will be read." The American press covered Bodenheim's last blaze of notoriety, and periodicals such as Moscow's *Literary Gazette* (*Literaturnaä Gazeta*) also noted his passing. The February 11 issue of the Moscow magazine mentioned especially that he "joined the battle of the jobless" during the 1930's, and that he had often "described the life of the poor" in his novels. The sympathetic article calls the scene of his death "America's wilderness district" and concludes that the poet was a "victim of the 'American way of life.'"

CHAPTER 7

Summation

A NY conclusions concerning Maxwell Bodenheim's contribution to American life and letters must mention his own life, since unfortunately that has so far been his major known contribution: Bodenheim as symbolic of the Bohemian free spirit or of some ancient obscene Huck Finn rebelling with whiskey on his breath against civilization. Bodenheim as myth perverts what he actually was: a talented and wretched man who added to whatever warping force he experienced as a young man his own bundle of self-destructive impulses. And perhaps his horrifying contribution to American life was best phrased by Louis Grudin in a eulogy he prepared for Bodenheim's funeral but was not asked to deliver: "A recent photo of his face tells more than anyone can say about Max. It is a ravaged, dying face. Everything that we fear is in that face. It has a noble structure, and it is in ruins . . . We shudder at the way he lived and the way he died. None of us, alone, could do anything about it. The difference between his condition and ours was slight; and now it is merely that the horror of *his* ordeal is more vividly apparent than ours."

As a critic, Bodenheim contributed a caustic, iconoclastic, highly individualized view of American civilization. He consistently opposed the sham-Freudianism of post-World War I literature; and, with taste no less sensitive than many of his now better-known contemporaries, he championed such writers as Hart Crane, John Dos Passos, Conrad Aiken, Wallace Stevens, Kenneth Fearing, and William Carlos Williams. Certainly the man whose "whole blooming book" on esthetics Ezra Pound wanted to publish, even though, as Pound wrote, only he and Samuel Putnam would understand it, deserves greater investigation.[1]

Bodenheim's fiction, though it clearly suffers from lack of technical skill and errors in diction, and from what Marianne Moore pinpointed in the September, 1924, *Dial* as his "interest in retaliation," contributed more to American literature than most slighting references to it indicate. *Blackguard* shows what it must have been like to be a young foolish poet in the early years of one of America's greatest literary periods. Works such as *Ninth Avenue* reveal the materialistic frauds and sexual hypocrisies in American life, and they also portray the individual struggle against a bleak and corrosive urban civilization to which man, to his own near-destruction has habituated himself. He exhibits an unfaltering ability to describe the viciousness and tedium of what he termed "upper proletarian" family life in its constant disintegration. Books such as *Crazy Man* and even the generally unsuccessful *Replenishing Jessica* show an exact touch in portraying the sick city's fourth and fifth raters—cheap comics, taxi dancers, fake artists. Often his sense of locale presents how it was in a dance hall like the Merry Grotto and how the metallic floors burned in a Memphis jail. He describes scenes eminently suited to their marginal inhabitants, the losers and *schlemiels,* the whores and jobless, the trapped outsiders of contemporary life. Occasionally, as in *Naked on Roller Skates* and in parts of *Blackguard* and *Duke Herring,* he wrote of modern city life comically, creating rough satire whose bludgeon sometimes concealed a fine point.

Stylistically, he could simply evoke the numbing torpor of Depression life as in *Slow Vision,* or impressionistically depict the exploding and then sputtering-out of a riot, as in *Run, Sheep, Run.* His critical prose could be cold and reasoned, as, for example, when defending free verse in his "Reply to A. C. H.," or comic and colorful, as in most of his work for the Chicago *Literary Times.* And no style but Bodenheim's would describe the effect of poison in the blood of a beautiful girl as he did in "The Master Poisoner": "The skin becomes a milk-tinted pond, in which wine-ghosts timidly bathe."

In "American Novels," Bodenheim wrote that the novel should be "more concerned with inward investigation and less immersed with outward, colloquial and visual fidelities." His major difficulty as a novelist is perhaps that he never achieved a completely adequate technique for presenting the "inward investigation." Yet where he apparently did not care to succeed, "with outward, colloquial and visual fidelities," he had significant potential as novelist. Even relatively doctrinaire books like *Slow Vision* and *Run, Sheep, Run* show an ability to root ideas in realistic detail.

Bodenheim's achievements in poetry are, however, more constant and definite than his achievements in prose. Each of his successive volumes has its flaws, but each offers at least three or four poems of high value that arrest the reader's attention and make him linger over lines and phrases, that offer a variety of poetry no one else, precisely, was writing. "Death," "Seaweed from Mars," "Rattle-Snake Mountain Fable I," "Summer Evening: New York Subway Station," "Platonic Narrative," "Fairy-Tale," "Bringing Jazz," and "Dear Noel Coward" are only a random handful of Bodenheim's poems that deserve attention. These are intensely his own. He worked in his own stylistic areas and, for good or bad, presented his unique manner and vision.

He also achieved variety in the nature of his poetry. His work was esoteric, and popular; made no compromises to public taste; and dealt with materials springing directly from the public domain. He wrote fragile and erotic love poems; tender realistic and naturalistic poems of urban life; poems describing imaginary worlds of mind and matter; jazz poems; humorous poems; and poems whose commentary on history (such as the war poems) are horrifying; and he wrote poems of art's independence and of art's social obligations. His accomplishment in these areas is uneven: everything he did was uneven. His esthetic, as expressed in "Esthetics, Criticism, and Life" almost guarantees unevenness: "etshetics recognizes laws of the moment" only; is "unruly"; shows "disorder."

But, from the outset of his career, he was not content to view poetry narrowly, and so he incorporated much of his own person and his own interests at any one time into his work and had also perhaps a great need and urge to let the poetry justify the life, so that the craft of his poetry became somewhat neglected in the poetry's self-involvement. To him, the self was not narrow but very broad; unfortunately for his work and life, he himself was chaotically organized. His gift for phrasing and his keen original intellect, properly disciplined and cautiously focused, might have produced a skilled craftsman of high order—but discipline and caution could have also produced a bland journeyman, which Bodenheim certainly was not. He was an interesting and often striking poet.

I believe it true of Bodenheim's life and art that rarely has an American writer of any historic significance committed more obvious and sometimes more disastrous mistakes: but it is also true that rarely have the virtues and the accomplishments of such a writer been so clearly misrepresented and so quickly forgotten.

Notes and References

I have tried to eliminate footnotes wherever possible without confusing the reader. Much of my biographical information comes from personal interviews and uncollected letters, and I have tried to cross-check this material. Nearly all the letters I quote from are in private collections inaccessible at this time to the general student. When I could, I dated these letters.

Chapter One

1. Here as elsewhere, Bodenheim's first wife, Minna, supplied helpful details. Floyd Dell was one of several to mention to me Bodenheim's self-destructive tendencies. Dell has never published on Bodenheim, but he wrote me several letters.

2. *Sherwood Anderson's Memoirs* (New York, 1942), p. 199; Margaret Anderson, *My Thirty Year's War* (New York, 1930), pp. 53, 193; Emma Goldman, *Living My Life* (Garden City, New York, 1934), p. 532.

3. Harriet Monroe, "Maxwell Bodenheim," *Poetry*, XXV (March, 1925), 320.

4. Bodenheim's handwritten manuscripts are in incredibly tiny writing. Some of his pages look like solid pencil marks and can be read only with a magnifying glass.

5. Lawrence Langner, *The Magic Curtain* (Toronto, 1952), p. 86.

6. Margaret Anderson, p. 53.

7. Alfred Kreymborg, in *Troubadour* (New York, 1925), mentions Bodenheim throughout its text. All quotations from Kreymborg, except his remarks at Bodenheim's funeral, are from this source.

8. All Pound quotations except one in my "Summation" are from *The Letters of Ezra Pound, 1907–1941*, ed. by D. D. Paige (New York, 1950). The book contains a complete index. William Troy, "The Story of the Little Magazines," *Bookman*, LXX (February, 1930), 659.

9. *The Selected Letters of William Carlos Williams*, ed. by John Thirlwall (New York, 1957), p. 37.

10. The quotations are from *The Letters of Hart Crane*, ed. by Brom Weber (New York, 1952). Phillip Horton's biography of Crane (New York, 1937) contains similar information. Crane also wrote a generally positive review of *Minna and Myself* in *The Pagan*, III (February, 1919), pp. 59–60.

11. Harriet Monroe, *A Poet's Life* (New York, 1938), p. 413.

12. Arthur and Barbara Gelb, *O'Neill* (New York, 1960), p. 361.

13. Kenneth Rexroth, "In Old Chicago," *Show*, LV (July–August, 1964), p. 69.

14. Bodenheim was no draft-dodger, despite some legends that have circulated to the contrary. His prior record removed him from the draft. In *Crazy Man*, his hero remembers with anger not being allowed to enlist because of his jail record.

15. "Counterpoint and Implication," *Poetry*, XIV (June, 1919), p. 153.

16. *Collected Essays of John Peale Bishop*, ed. by Edmund Wilson (New York, 1948), p. 274; Cowley, "Euphues," *Dial*, LXXIII (October, 1922), p. 446; Sapir, review of *Introducing Irony*, *Nation*, CXIV (June 21, 1922), p. 751.

17. *Letters of H. L. Mencken*, ed. by Guy J. Forgue (New York, 1961), p. 250.

18. Edmund Wilson, *A Literary Chronicle* (Garden City, New York, 1956), p. 87. The essay was originally written in 1926.

19. See for example the anonymous review of *Duke Herring* in *Saturday Review of Literature*, LXXIV (September, 1931), lv.

20. Bodenheim's remarks are quoted in Duffey's *The Chicago Renaissance in American Letters* (East Lansing, 1954), p. 255.

Chapter Two

1. Conrad Aiken, "Vox—et Praetera," *Dial*, LXVI, pp. 356–57. Mr. Aiken has also written several brief notes to me about Bodenheim's poetry and life.

2. Letter to Conrad Aiken, April 7, 1918.

3. Letter to me, January 14, 1965. Bodenheim wrote several stories of spectral appearances, including "Psychic Phenomena" in *Introducing Irony*, which dramatizes an experience he said was his.

4. Letter to Aiken, April 7, 1918.

5. "Modern Poetry," *Dial*, LXVIII (January, 1920), p. 95.

6. "What Is Poetry?" *New Republic*, XIII (December, 1917), p. 24.

7. "Modern Poetry," *Dial*, p. 97.

8. "A Reply to A. C. H.," *Poetry*, XIV (June, 1919), p. 172.

9. *Letters of Robert Frost to Louis Untermeyer*, ed. by Louis Untermeyer (New York, 1963), p. 106.

10. Undated letter headed "'Thursday eve. love to Solbert'"; *Nation*, CXIX (October 8, 1924), p. 373.

11. Poe's "Hans Pfall" and "Mesmeric Revelation" probably influenced the poem also, in depicting extremes of hot and cold, particles of thought, and the disparate apprehension of substances in various planets.

12. René Taupin, *L'Influence du Symbolisme* (Paris, 1929), pp. 270, 272.

13. The book's first half employs autobiographic material drawn from Bodenheim's family relationships and his years of wandering. The second half contains autobiographic reminiscences of Bodenheim's sweetheart Fedya, and portraits of Harriet Monroe and Margaret Anderson. Miss Anderson apparently had greater influence over the young poet, if *Blackguard* can be accepted as evidence.

14. I am indebted for the Dewey quotation and for several issues it raises to Richard Mitchell, "Studs Lonigan: Research in Morality," *Centennial Review*, VI (Spring, 1962), pp. 202–14.

15. Bodenheim frequently used real people as prototypes for his characters. Carley is in many ways similar to Bodenheim's friend John Coffee (or Coffey). Both employed the same technique of thieving, for example.

16. With greater discipline, Bodenheim could have supported himself either as a journalist or, as the quoted passage shows, an advertising writer. Those of his friends who did one or the other were usually mocked by him.

17. The composer Douglas Moore and George M. Kendall, General Director of the MacDowell Association, have graciously provided me with information on Bodenheim's stays at the Colony. Margaret Widdemer's *Golden Friends I Had* contains several comic memories of Bodenheim in Peterborough.

Chapter Three

1. Several versions of the dog story exist. One is in Horace Gregory, *Portrait of the Poet in Her Time* (New York, 1958), pp. 167–69; another is in Louis Untermeyer's *From Another World* (New York, 1939), pp. 103–4.

2. Information on Bodenheim's sensational escapades of this period are generally from Allen Churchill's *The Improper Bohemians* (New York, 1959); Albert Parry's *A History of Bohemianism in America* (New York, 1960); and from a few personal interviews with his first wife, with one of his publishers, and with some of his intimates who prefer anonymity.

3. I have not seen the manuscript *Replenishing Jessica*. I have seen other manuscripts of Bodenheim's work, and in these, nothing of a sexual nature exists that a publisher would want to cut on grounds of alleged pornography.

4. The best adverse criticism of the novel—in fact the best adverse criticism of Bodenheim's fiction—is S. J. Perelman's parody "Cloudland Revisited," *New Yorker*, XXV (July 9, 1949).

5. My discussion of the American city novel is clearly indebted to Blanche Housman Gelfant, *The American City Novel* (Norman, Oklahoma; 1954). Professor Gelfant does not discuss Bodenheim, however.

Chapter Four

1. Aaron Sussman, "Trade Winds," *Saturday Review of Literature,* XXXVI (March 13, 1954), pp. 5–8.
2. "The Demonic Quest," *Recent American Fiction,* ed. by Joseph J. Waldmeir (Boston, 1963), p. 62.
3. I have seen "Bringing Jazz" performed successfully several times in this manner.
4. Ellipses in *Bringing Jazz!* poems are Bodenheim's, except where noted.

Chapter Six

1. Daniel Aaron, *Writers on the Left* (New York, 1961); Walter B. Rideout, *The Radical Novel in the United States* (Cambridge, 1956).
2. E. S. Fergotson, "The New Line and the Old Bottle," *Poetry,* LX (July, 1942), p. 220.
3. In a manuscript poem never published, supplied me by Louis Grudin, Bodenheim indicated the problems of his own "search": he could never be quite sure of his allegiance. The poem is titled "Lenin" and reads in part "The revolution tore his breast—/ Slaughter, slaughter, draw and quarter, soak the earth with blushing milk,/ Who kills a man kills all of life. . . ./ You were a wise man and a fool,/ Lenin—a truck horse and a stunted poet/ Smashing harness, stamping earth/ To gallop to the top." (Ellipsis mine.)
4. A letter of Bodenheim's to Horace Gregory suggests Bodenheim's fallen reputation at this stage in his career. "This poem had been definitely accepted by *New Masses* 2½ months ago, and because of its timeliness—Coward's auto-biography *Present Indicative* came out this year— [Joseph] Freeman promised to make every effort to print it. . . . Alexander Taylor repeated the promise . . . and the next thing I heard was that this 'accepted' poem had been sent to you for your decision." Some magazines, such as *Hound and Horn* now sent him standard printed rejection slips with no comment. *Poetry,* which he inundated with poems almost until his death, was always kind and receptive to him, even when it did not accept his work.
5. Joseph Mitchell, "Joe Gould's Secret," *New Yorker* (September 26, 1964), p. 92. Bodenheim met the younger eccentrics as well. Jack

Kerouac reported to me that he, Bodenheim, and Allan Ginsberg were thrown out of Bodenheim's rooming-house hallway once for making too much noise.

Chapter Seven

1. Unpublished letter from Ezra Pound to Samuel Putnam.

Selected Bibliography

PRIMARY SOURCES

Novels
A Virtuous Girl, New York: H. Liveright, 1930.
Blackguard. Chicago: Covici-McGee, 1923.
Crazy Man. New York: Harcourt, Brace, 1924.
Duke Herring. New York: H. Liveright, 1931.
Georgie May. New York: Boni and Liveright, 1928.
Naked on Roller Skates. H. Liveright, 1930.
New York Madness. New York: The Macauley Company, 1933.
Ninth Avenue. New York: Boni and Liveright, 1926.
Replenishing Jessica. New York: Boni and Liveright, 1925.
Run, Sheep, Run. New York: H. Liveright, 1932.
6 A.M. New York: H. Liveright, 1932. (Neither myself nor Professor DeVoe has been able to locate a copy of this book, which is listed in the *Cumulative Book Index*.)
Sixty Seconds. New York: H. Liveright, 1929.
Slow Vision. New York: The Macauley Company, 1934.

Poetry
Advice. New York: Knopf, 1920.
Against This Age. New York: Boni and Liveright, 1923.
Bringing Jazz! New York: H. Liveright, 1930.
Introducing Irony. New York: Boni and Liveright, 1922.
The King of Spain. New York: Boni and Liveright, 1928.
Lights in the Valley. New York: Harbinger, 1942.
Minna and Myself. New York: Pagan Publishing Co., 1918.
Returning to Emotion. New York. Boni and Liveright, 1927.
The Sardonic Arm. Chicago: Covici-McGee, 1923.
Selected Poems. New York: Beechhurst Press, Bernard Ackerman, 1946.
Seven Poets in Search of an Answer: A Poetic Symposium. Ed. by Thomas Yoseleff. New York: Bernard Ackerman, 1944.

Critical Articles (Only a few representative pieces are listed)
"American Novels." *Saturday Review of Literature*, III (March 26, 1927), 673–74.
"Candidly Speaking." *Literary Review*, III (January 27, 1923), 409–10.
Chicago Literary Times, I and II (March 1, 1923–June 1, 1924), *passim*.

"Criticism in America." *Saturday Review of Literature*, I (June 6, 1925), 801–2.

"Esthetics, Criticism, and Life." *The New Review*, I (January–February, 1931), 1–9.

"Men and Women." *Dial*, LXVIII (May, 1920), 562–64.

"Modern Poetry." *Dial*, LXVIII (January, 1920), 95–98.

"On Literary Groups." *American Mercury*, III (October, 1924), 206–8.

"Psychoanalysis and American Fiction." *Nation*, CXIV (June 7, 1922), 683–84.

"A Reply to A. C. H." *Poetry*, XIV (June, 1919), 170–73.

"The Revolutionary Poet." *Little Magazine*, I (February–March, 1934). I have been unable to discover the page number.

"Roughneck and Romancer." *O'Neill and His Plays*. Ed. by Oscar Cargill *et al.* New York: New York University Press, 1961.

"Self-Glorification and Art." *Dial*, LXVIII (January, 1921), 92–94.

"Tendencies in Modern Poetry and Prose." *North American Review*, CCXII (April, 1921), 551–55.

"Truth and Realism in Literature." *Nation*, CXIX (October 8, 1924), 373.

"What Is Poetry?" *New Republic*, XIII (December 22, 1917), 211–12.

Miscellaneous

Bodenheim recorded a number of his poems for the Library of Congress. The tape is LWO 2529. *American Literary Manuscripts* lists several collections of Bodenheim material. The great bulk of his letters and manuscripts are still in private hands. The New York Public Library theater collection, now housed at the Lincoln Center for the Performing Arts, in New York City, has several manuscript plays. *Cutie, a Warm Mama*, written in collaboration with Ben Hecht, is a novella published privately by the Hechtshaw Press, Chicago, 1924. Only two hundred copies were printed. *My Life and Loves in Greenwich Village*, New York: Bridgehead Books, 1954, cannot be attributed to Bodenheim, though his name is listed on the cover as author. External and internal evidence makes Bodenheim's authorship highly dubious.

SECONDARY SOURCES

Only items of especial interest or significance are listed. No full-length or chapter-length book analyses of Bodenheim exist, beyond Professor DeVoe's unpublished dissertation. Biographical information on Bodenheim is often anecdotal and fragmentary, and it should always be checked for accuracy.

AARON DANIEL. *Writers on the Left*. New York: Harcourt, Brace and

World, Inc. 1961. Contains very little on Bodenheim, but is excellent on left-wing writers and their times.

AIKEN CONRAD. *Conversation,* in *The Collected Novels of Conrad Aiken,* New York: Holt, Rinehart and Winston, 1964. Interesting and perceptive portrait of Bodenheim in his early thirties, suggesting both his artistry and personal disorganization.

——. "Counterpoint and Implication," *Poetry,* XIV (June, 1919), 152–59. Aiken praises Bodenheim's aims, contrasting them with the solid, unsoaring work of Edgar Lee Masters.

——. "Vox—et Praeterea," *Dial,* LXVI (April 5, 1919), 356–57. One of the best of the early Bodenheim reviews. Bodenheim read the review and by letter debated it with Aiken.

ANDERSON MARGARET. *My Thirty Year's War.* New York: Covici-Friede, 1930. Anecdotal comments by a woman who, according to *Blackguard,* exerted a great personal influence over the young poet.

BISHOP, JOHN PEALE. *The Collected Essays of John Peale Bishop.* Ed. by Edmund Wilson. New York: Charles Scribner's Sons, 1948. Reprints Bishop's *Vanity Fair* review of *Introducing Irony,* a perceptive if ultimately uncommitted criticism of Bodenheim's poetic virtues and vices.

BRAITHWAITE, WILLIAM STANLEY. *Anthology of American Verse for 1926.* Boston: B. J. Brimmer, Co., 1927. Good for a standard, official, popular view of Bodenheim's midcareer. His significance is noted in three separate articles.

CHURCHILL, ALLEN. *The Improper Bohemians.* New York: E. P. Dutton and Company, 1959. Well-written account of Bodenheim's Village milieu, and of several sensational Bodenheim escapades.

COWLEY, MALCOLM. "Euphues," *Dial,* LXXVII (October, 1922), 446–48. Examines Bodenheim as an exotic, talented, if often disappointing poet.

CRANE, HART. *The Letters of Hart Crane.* Ed. by Brom Weber. New York: Hermitage House, 1952. The young Crane praises Bodenheim; the older Crane does not.

DAY, DOROTHY. *Loaves and Fishes.* New York: Harper and Row, 1963. A very moving account of Bodenheim's last few years and his relationship with Ruth.

DEUTSCH, HELEN, and HANAU, STELLA. *The Provincetown, A Story of the Theatre.* New York: Farrar and Rinehart, Inc., 1931. Interesting details concerning Bodenheim's connections with the young theatrical company.

DEVOE, EDWARD T. "A Soul in Gaudy Tatters: A Critical Biography of Maxwell Bodenheim." Unpublished doctoral dissertation, Pennsylvania State University, 1957. A very good ground-breaking study.

DUFFEY, BERNARD. *The Chicago Renaissance in American Letters*. East Lansing: The Michigan State College Press, 1954. Definitive study of the movement in which Bodenheim played a small but interesting role.

FERGOTSON, E. S. "The New Line and the Old Bottle," *Poetry*, LX (July, 1942), 219–23. A critic not of Bodenheim's generation extinguishes *Lights in the Valley*. Interesting to compare with early reviews by Bodenheim's contemporaries.

HECHT, BEN. *A Child of the Century*. New York: Simon and Schuster, 1954.

———. *Count Bruga*. New York: Horace Liveright, 1926.

———. *Gaily, Gaily*. Garden City, New York: Doubleday and Company, 1963.

———. *Letters From Bohemia*. Garden City, New York: Doubleday and Company, 1964.

———. *1001 Afternoons in New York*. New York: The Viking Press, 1941. These are a few of the works in which Hecht mentions Bodenheim. All are interestingly written and contain some truth, and all are partly journalistic creations.

KLONSKY, MILTON, "Squash and Stretch," *Esquire*, LX (December, 1963), 162 *passim*. Bodenheim as a Village legend. Very inaccurate.

KREYMBORG, ALFRED. *Troubadour*. New York: Liveright, Inc., 1925. A delightfully written account of Bodenheim's arrival on the New York scene, and a good anecdotal account of pre-1920 poetry.

LANGNER, LAWRENCE. *The Magic Curtain*. Toronto: George Harrap and Co., Ltd., 1952. Comic remembrance of young Bodenheim caught between the Scylla and Charybdis of Harriet Monroe and Margaret Anderson.

"The Literary Life," *Time*, LIX (February 18, 1952), 21. Droll account of Bodenheim as a decaying bum.

MONROE, HARRIET. "Comment, Maxwell Bodenheim," *Poetry*, XXV March, 1925), 320–27. Praises Bodenheim, but wonders about his future. Questions what embitters him so.

———. *A Poet's Life*. New York: The Macmillan Company, 1938. Anecdotal reminiscence of a relatively innocent, young Bodenheim that rarely appears elsewhere.

MOORE, MARIANNE. "Thistles Dipped in Frost," *Dial*, LXXVII (September, 1924), 251–52. Sensitive and blunt review of *Crazy Man*, which admits Bodenheim's high status as writer, but questions his future as novelist.

"Murder in Bohemia," *Life*, XXXVI (February 22, 1954), 39. Lurid pictorial account of Bodenheim's death. The February 15 issues of *Time* and *Newsweek* also carried short articles and obituaries.

PARRY, ALBERT. *A History of Bohemianism in America* (revised ed.). New York: Dover Publications, 1960. Standard work on the subject, with some anecdotes of Bodenheim in Chicago and New York.

PERELMAN, S. J. "Cloudland Revisited," *New Yorker*, XXV (July 9, 1949), 16–18. Excellent criticism, through comic retelling, of *Replenishing Jessica*.

Poetry, LXXXIV (May, 1954), 123. Sympathetic obituary of Bodenheim, stressing his connections with the magazine.

POUND, EZRA. *The Letters of Ezra Pound, 1907–1941*. Ed. by D. D. Paige. New York: Harcourt, Brace and World, Inc., 1950. Sporadic references are made to Bodenheim, whom Pound often thought well of.

TAUPIN RENE. *L'Influence du Symbolisme Français sur La Poésie Americaine*. Paris: Librairie Ancienne Honore Champion, 1929. Generally negative criticism by a French critic who seems bothered that Bodenheim was not Baudelaire.

Index